Everyday Favourites

Everyday Favourites

VANYA INSULL

ALLEN&UNWIN
SYDNEY • MELBOURNE • AUCKLAND • LONDON

For my husband, Mike,
and our amazing boys,
Archie and Henry

Contents

Introduction

First of all, thanks so much for choosing my cookbook and for joining me on this journey. I'm sure you're going to love the recipe selection — the book is packed full of my fresh and tasty favourites; all super-easy to adapt to your family's tastes and so yummy that they'll even impress those fussy kids.

I created this book to serve as your food bible — the one cookbook you can't do without — and I'm so proud of what it's become. I firmly believe that cooking for a family doesn't have to be hard or intimidating, and my goal is to help you gain confidence in the kitchen.

In these pages you'll find easy everyday recipes that the whole family will enjoy, using affordable ingredients. Once you master these recipes and have them in your regular rotation, you can't go wrong, and I know you'll return to them over and over again. It gives me great joy to imagine your copy of this book covered in food splatters from all the delicious food you'll be cooking with it.

The book is simple to navigate, with five chapters covering all your needs. 'Light Meals' are breezy, flavourful lunches or dinners for when you need something quick and not too heavy. 'Everyday Dinners' are your midweek go-tos when you're feeding a hungry family, and the 'Winter Warmers'

chapter is for slow-cooked meats and heart-warming stews. Most of my dinner recipes are freezer-friendly, because I like to make big batches and freeze the extra portions for later. That way, you've always got a meal on hand that you can whip up (or repurpose as a filling or topping for wraps, pizza or baked potatoes).

Let's not forget the sweet side of life. My 'Home Baking' chapter is full of scrumptious cakes, loaves and breads that are perfect for taking along to a morning or afternoon tea. And 'Sweet Treats' features some of my most popular slices and cookies, sure to satisfy any cravings you may have.

My two boys' favourite recipes have been identified throughout the book, so look for the *Kids' Fave* sticker if you are cooking for little ones. You can also get your youngsters to check out the pictures at the start of each chapter and suggest a recipe they'd like you to try. They'll love the responsibility of choosing from a 'menu'!

You may wonder how this whirlwind started for me and how I became so obsessed with food. Perhaps you have followed me on Instagram or Facebook, where I have an amazing community and audience. Many of my followers have been begging me for a real-life cookbook. So, if that's you, thanks for the encouragement and I hope you're enjoying having this baby in your hands!

Growing up, I was quite a fussy eater, and it might surprise you to learn that I wasn't keen on much flavour at all. Mum would serve up a carbonara and I would ask for plain pasta with salt! But all that changed when I landed my first job out of university, as a junior designer at *Taste* magazine. At 22, I found myself going along to photo shoots and working with amazing cooks and a talented team to design a beautiful magazine — and that's where my love of food began. Looking at all those delicious plates of food and reading the recipes inspired me, and soon I was becoming more adventurous in my own food choices and my cooking.

My career in the magazine industry kept me busy and I worked on a number of women's and food magazines, eventually returning to the *Taste* team as an art director — which meant attending a lot more photo shoots and taking responsibility for the design and look of the magazine.

Life changed again in 2016, when our youngest child was six months old. My husband Mike and I decided to sell our house in Auckland and move to beautiful Lake Taupō in the middle of New Zealand, and we have never looked back. In Taupō I had more free time, and I started documenting what I was cooking by making little videos. Soon I had set up a Facebook page called VJ Cooks, which I used to share my recipe creations with friends and family.

The videos on the page started getting traction, and in December that year I had a few recipes for Christmas desserts that were wildly popular. I thought to myself, *Hey, I could make something of this.* So I began to produce a new recipe video every few weeks. Then I posted a video where I made my aunty's chocolate Weet-Bix slice and it went viral, reaching a million views in a few months.

From there my Facebook page grew quickly, and I set up an Instagram profile as well. I continued developing easy family recipes for my followers, and when Instagram Stories came out I filmed myself cooking dinner almost every evening. I was just experimenting a lot of the time, but people seemed to love watching; enjoying my successes — and sometimes my failures, too!

By this stage I had built up a substantial library of recipes and I needed a website to share them all on, so I launched my website vjcooks.com. It now has more than 300 recipes and has become a go-to for home cooks on the hunt for fuss-free dinners, baking and desserts.

Fast-forward a few years — and hundreds of recipes — and my Facebook and Instagram pages are still growing . . . and these days I'm on Pinterest, YouTube and even TikTok!

So that's a little bit about me and my journey. I love food and I think about it all day long, and it makes me so happy to picture you all making the recipes in this cookbook. I know that you're going to love them as much as I do. If you're on Instagram or Facebook please give me a tag, because you know I'll be there to spot it and share it! Seeing people recreate my recipes really is the highlight of my day.

Happy cooking!

VJ x

About My Recipes

As a busy mum, I design my recipes to take the stress out of feeding a family. I try to keep them as simple as possible, using everyday ingredients that you probably already have in the pantry or fridge — and that your kids are likely to be happy to eat!

A lot of my dinner recipes are super-versatile, and I've often provided tips to suggest substitute ingredients or serving suggestions. Feel free to add or swap in any appropriate vegetables that you have hiding in the back of your fridge.

While most of my dinner recipes feed a family of four, a few of the winter meals and pulled meats make a larger quantity because I like to freeze extra portions for another meal at a later date. Once the leftovers have cooled to room temperature, I transfer them to an airtight container or sealable bag and freeze them for up to 3 months. When I need a meal in a hurry, I defrost them and reheat until piping hot, then use in tacos, nachos, wedges, burgers, baked potatoes, or even on top of pizza.

I also love to freeze baking to have on hand for a quick lunchbox filler. Cookie dough, muffins and loaves all freeze well, so I often double the recipes. I also freeze pizza dough to have ready for a last-minute dinner.

I use fan bake for the majority of my cooking, unless stated otherwise. If you are using a conventional oven instead, the general rule of thumb is to add 20°C (70°F), so for example 180°C (350°F) fan bake would be 200°C (400°F) in a conventional oven.

All ovens have their own quirks. You probably already know if yours runs hot or cold, so feel free to adjust the cook times and temperatures accordingly.

When baking, I always line my tins and trays with baking paper. This prevents my baking from sticking to the tin and ensures everything comes out in one piece. It also makes for an easy clean-up.

I specify the size of my baking tins in my recipes, but if your tins are slightly different they will still work! If your tin is larger the bake time will be shorter, whereas if it's smaller it may take longer for your baking to fully cook through. Just keep an eye on the cooking time and bake until it is cooked through and a skewer comes out clean.

MASTER MEASUREMENTS

I use New Zealand standard measures in my recipes:

1 teaspoon = 5 ml (⅙ fl oz)

1 tablespoon = 15 ml (½ fl oz)

¼ cup of liquid = 60 ml (2 fl oz)

½ cup of liquid = 125 ml (4 fl oz)

1 cup of liquid = 250 ml (9 fl oz)

The weight of a cup of dry ingredients will vary depending on the mass of the ingredients. These are some of the common quantities I use in my baking and this cookbook:

1 cup of flour = 150 g (5½ oz)

1 cup of wholemeal flour = 155 g (5⅔ oz)

1 cup of white or caster sugar = 220 g (7¾ oz)

1 cup of brown sugar (firmly packed) = 200 g (7 oz)

1 cup of icing sugar = 130 g (4½ oz)

1 cup of cocoa = 90 g (3¼ oz)

1 cup of grated cheese = 100 g (3½ oz)

Light Meals

What's in this Chapter

EASY SPINACH AND FETA TART • **PAGE 30**

HALOUMI, BACON AND CORN ORZO SALAD • **PAGE 32**

GRILLED STEAK AND FETA PITA POCKETS • **PAGE 34**

MY CLASSIC PASTA SALAD • **PAGE 36**

MY FAVOURITE DRESSINGS AND SAUCES • **PAGES 38–42**

Corn Fritter and Bacon Stack

We love corn fritters in our house, and these ones are packed with protein from the cottage cheese. Serve them stacked with avo and bacon and you have one delicious breakfast, lunch or even dinner!

2 eggs
400 g (14 oz) can corn
  kernels, drained
250 g (9 oz) cottage cheese
½ cup grated cheese
½ cup milk
1 spring onion, finely sliced
2 Tbsp chopped fresh
  parsley
1½ cups self-raising flour
salt and cracked black
  pepper, to taste
1 Tbsp olive oil

TO SERVE
250 g (9 oz) streaky bacon,
  grilled or fried until crispy
flesh of 2 avocados, sliced
½ cup sour cream
¼ cup sweet chilli sauce

1. Whisk the eggs in a large bowl. Stir in the corn, cottage cheese, cheese, milk, spring onion and parsley.

2. Add the flour and mix until there are no lumps. Season well with salt and pepper.

3. Heat the oil in a large non-stick frying pan over a medium heat. Working in batches, add ¼ cup scoops of mixture, spreading evenly to about 10 cm (4 in) in diameter.

4. Turn the fritters over when they are crisp and golden on the bottom. When both sides are cooked, remove from the pan and keep warm in the oven while you fry the next batch. You should have 12 fritters.

5. Stack 3 corn fritters on each plate. Serve topped with crispy bacon, sliced avocado, sour cream and sweet chilli sauce.

TIPS AND TRICKS
+ *Chopped feta would work well as a substitute for grated cheese.*
+ *Leave out the bacon to make this a vegetarian meal.*

Kids'
fave

Cheesy Ham and Tomato Crustless Quiche

A light, crustless quiche filled with the winning combination of ham, cheese and tomato, this is a great dish to serve as a light meal with a side salad or greens. It's also good served cold the next day at a picnic, or as a lunchbox filler. The recipe is versatile, so you can add or swap in zucchini, carrot, spinach, silver beet, mushrooms, bacon, salami or cooked potatoes.

4 eggs
½ cup milk
1 cup grated cheese
¾ cup plain flour
100 g (3½ oz) ham, diced
2 spring onions, finely sliced
1 tsp baking powder
½ tsp salt
¼ tsp cracked black pepper
100 g (3½ oz) cherry
  tomatoes, halved

1. Preheat the oven to 180°C (350°F) fan bake.

2. Whisk the eggs in a large bowl, then mix in the milk.

3. Add all the remaining ingredients except the tomatoes, and stir together.

4. Transfer to a greased or lined quiche dish or small baking dish and spread out evenly. Arrange the halved tomatoes on top.

5. Bake for 40 minutes until golden and cooked through. Allow to sit in the dish for about 10 minutes before serving.

TIPS AND TRICKS

+ *Swap the plain flour for gluten-free flour if you prefer.*

Crispy Fish Burgers with Home-made Tartare Sauce

We love fishing in the summer holidays, and whenever we catch fresh snapper or gurnard I make these burgers. The home-made tartare sauce takes them to the next level, and the combination of butter and oil when frying makes the fish extra crispy.

---

4 firm white fish fillets
3 Tbsp plain flour
1 egg
½ cup panko crumbs
2 Tbsp sesame seeds
salt and cracked black
  pepper, to taste
1 Tbsp olive oil
1 Tbsp butter

TARTARE SAUCE
¼ cup mayonnaise
2 Tbsp finely chopped
  capers
2 small gherkins, finely
  chopped
1 spring onion, finely sliced
2 Tbsp lemon juice

TO SERVE
4 large burger buns
¼ iceberg lettuce, shredded
2 tomatoes, sliced
½ red onion, finely sliced
  (optional)

1. To make the Tartare Sauce, mix all the ingredients in a small bowl. Chill until ready to serve.

2. Put the fish fillets and flour in a plastic bag and shake until coated. Crack in the egg and shake again until coated.

3. Mix together the panko crumbs, sesame seeds, salt and pepper on a plate. Coat the fish with the crumb mixture on both sides.

4. Heat the oil and butter in a large frying pan over a medium-high heat. Add the fish and cook on both sides until golden and cooked through, adjusting the heat as necessary to prevent the butter from burning.

5. Cut the buns in half and grill or toast until warm. Spread the Tartare Sauce on each bun, then fill with the lettuce, crispy fish, tomato and red onion (if using). Add another dollop of sauce, if desired.

TIPS AND TRICKS
+ *Gurnard, snapper, tarakihi and blue cod would all work well in this recipe. You'll need about 500 g (1 lb 2 oz) for four people.*
+ *You can prepare the fish and tartare earlier in the day and chill them until you are ready to cook at dinner time.*

Crispy Bacon and Pesto Potato Salad

This crowd-pleasing salad is fit for any occasion. The creamy pesto dressing goes so well with the crispy bacon and perfectly boiled potatoes. If you take this to a potluck, I guarantee someone will ask you for the recipe.

150 g (5½ oz) streaky bacon
1 kg (2 lb 4 oz) baby
  potatoes, halved
1 tsp salt
½ cup sour cream
½ cup thick mayonnaise
¼ cup pesto
¼ cup chopped sun-dried
  tomatoes
1 Tbsp capers
1 handful fresh basil

1. Grill or fry the bacon until crispy. Allow to cool, then cut into bite-sized pieces.

2. Place the potatoes and salt in a large pot, cover with water and bring to a gentle simmer over a medium heat. Cook for 15–20 minutes until tender when pierced with a fork.

3. Drain, return to the pot, then add the sour cream, mayonnaise, pesto, sun-dried tomatoes and half the crispy bacon. Mix together.

4. Transfer to a serving dish and scatter with the remaining bacon. Garnish with capers and basil.

5. Serve warm or chill until ready to serve. It will keep well in an airtight container in the fridge for up to 2 days.

TIPS AND TRICKS

+ *The bacon can be grilled if you prefer, but frying it makes it a little crispier.*

Hot-smoked Salmon and Potato Frittata

A frittata is a super-easy and versatile dish, perfect served with a green salad for brunch or as a light dinner, and a great way to use up leftover potatoes. In this recipe you start out with the frying pan on the stovetop and finish off cooking the frittata under the grill until it is golden and cooked through. The hot-smoked salmon, capers and lemon zest are balanced out nicely by the creamy eggs and potatoes.

400 g (14 oz) potatoes, boiled
6 eggs
½ cup cream
1 Tbsp finely chopped capers
1 Tbsp finely grated lemon zest
1 Tbsp chopped fresh parsley
½ tsp salt
¼ tsp cracked black pepper
1 cup grated cheese
125 g (4½ oz) hot-smoked salmon

1. Preheat the oven to 200°C (400°F) fan grill.

2. Chop the cooked potatoes into bite-sized pieces.

3. Whisk together the eggs, cream, capers, lemon zest, parsley, salt and pepper. Stir in the cheese.

4. Place a large, well-seasoned ovenproof cast-iron frying pan over a medium heat. Arrange the potatoes evenly over the base of the pan, then pour over the egg mixture.

5. Gently flake the hot-smoked salmon and scatter it over the top. Without stirring, leave the pan on the stovetop to gently cook through.

6. Once the outside edge of the frittata turns lighter in colour, place the whole pan under the grill for 10 minutes until cooked through and golden on top.

7. Allow to rest in the pan for 10 minutes before serving.

TIPS AND TRICKS

+ *If you don't have a well-seasoned cast-iron frying pan, a regular ovenproof pan will work. Just use a drizzle of oil before adding the potatoes.*
+ *Any type of cheese will work in this recipe.*
+ *Frittata can also be served cold the next day.*

Quick Prawn Fried Rice

I always keep prawns in the freezer so I know I can whip up a quick, last-minute meal when I need to. This fried rice is packed full of flavour and the kids love it, too. If you aren't a fan of prawns, it's also delicious made with chicken or tofu.

---

1 Tbsp sesame oil
2 cups cooked white or
  brown rice
1 cup mixed frozen
  vegetables, thawed
2 eggs, whisked
2 Tbsp soy sauce
1 Tbsp oyster sauce
400 g (14 oz) raw prawns,
  thawed with tails removed
1 Tbsp sweet chilli sauce
1 spring onion, finely sliced
½ cup roasted cashew nuts

TO SERVE
1 handful fresh basil or
  coriander
Japanese mayonnaise
sriracha sauce (optional)

1. Heat the oil in a large frying pan over a medium heat. Add the cooked rice and stir-fry for a few minutes.

2. Stir in the mixed vegetables. Make a gap in the centre of the pan, pour in the eggs and let them cook like a mini omelette. Fold the egg over and use the end of the spatula to cut it into pieces.

3. Stir the soy sauce and oyster sauce into the rice and egg mixture. Add the prawns and sweet chilli sauce, and stir-fry until the prawns are pink and cooked through.

4. Add the spring onion and cashew nuts and stir together.

5. Serve hot, topped with basil or coriander, mayonnaise and sriracha (if using).

TIPS AND TRICKS
+ *The frozen vegetables I use are a mixture of carrot, corn and peas. You can also use fresh vegetables instead of frozen.*
+ *I like to serve my fried rice with a little bit of Japanese mayo and sriracha drizzled on top.*

Kids' fave

Easy Spinach and Feta Tart

Here, a crispy shortcrust case is filled with creamy eggs, spinach, sun-dried tomatoes and feta. Pair it with a green salad for an easy main meal, or it's just as delicious served cold for lunch or a picnic the next day. I always keep a bag of frozen spinach in the freezer, ready to add to recipes like this one.

2 sheets savoury shortcrust
   pastry
200 g (7 oz) frozen spinach
8 eggs
½ cup cream
2 Tbsp chopped fresh
   parsley or basil
¼ tsp salt
¼ tsp cracked black pepper
2 Tbsp finely chopped
   sun-dried tomatoes
100 g (3½ oz) feta
tomato relish or chutney,
   to serve

1. Preheat the oven to 180°C (350°F) fan bake.

2. Grease a 30 x 20 cm (12 x 8 in) tart tin with oil. Press the pastry sheets into the tin, overlapping where necessary to ensure the base and sides are covered. Prick the pastry with a fork, cover with baking paper then baking beads, and blind bake for 15 minutes.

3. Place the frozen spinach in a glass bowl and microwave for 1 minute. Transfer to a sieve and squeeze out any excess liquid.

4. Whisk together the eggs, cream, parsley or basil, salt and pepper. Stir in the spinach and sun-dried tomatoes.

5. Remove the crust from the oven. Pour in the egg mixture and crumble the feta over the top.

6. Bake for 30–35 minutes until golden and cooked through. Serve warm or cold with tomato relish or chutney.

Haloumi, Bacon and Corn Orzo Salad

This robust portable salad is ideal to take along to a barbecue or family get-together. It is quite a big salad, so it's perfect for meal prep at the start of the week. The combination of the bacon, corn and haloumi goes so well with the basil pesto and sun-dried tomatoes.

500 g (1lb 2 oz) orzo or risoni pasta
250 g (9 oz) streaky bacon
2 corn cobs, cooked
3 Tbsp pine nuts
200 g (7 oz) haloumi
3 Tbsp sliced sun-dried tomatoes
3 Tbsp chopped fresh basil

PESTO DRESSING
¼ cup pesto
1 Tbsp lemon juice
3 Tbsp olive oil

1. Cook the pasta according to the packet instructions until al dente. Drain and set aside.

2. Grill or fry the bacon until crispy. Allow to cool, then cut into bite-sized pieces.

3. Slice the kernels off the cooked corn cobs. Toast the pine nuts in a dry frying pan then set aside.

4. Cut the haloumi into 1 cm (½ in) slices and pan-fry for about 2 minutes on each side until golden. Cut into bite-sized pieces.

5. To make the Pesto Dressing, whisk together the pesto, lemon juice and olive oil.

6. Combine the cooked pasta, chopped bacon, corn kernels and sun-dried tomatoes in a large serving bowl. Add the dressing and mix everything together.

7. Serve topped with the fried haloumi, pine nuts and basil.

TIPS AND TRICKS
+ *Mix in some baby spinach, rocket or mesclun if you want to add more greens.*
+ *If you don't have pine nuts, you can dry-fry chopped walnuts or pumpkin seeds instead.*
+ *I love to use fresh corn when it's in season, but if you can't get it a cup of cooked frozen corn kernels will work too.*

Grilled Steak and Feta Pita Pockets

This is a great meal when you want dinner on the table fast. Cook the steak to your liking and make sure you rest it before slicing. Ready in around 20 minutes, it's just so easy.

400 g (14 oz) beef rump or
   sirloin steak
1 Tbsp olive oil
1 tsp paprika
salt and cracked black
   pepper, to taste

LEMON YOGHURT DRESSING
½ cup Greek yoghurt
¼ cucumber, finely diced
1 Tbsp lemon juice
1 Tbsp chopped fresh mint
salt and cracked black
   pepper, to taste

TO SERVE
4 large pita pockets
200 g (7 oz) cherry
   tomatoes, halved
50 g (1¾ oz) feta, crumbled
50 g (1¾ oz) baby spinach
flesh of 1 avocado, sliced

1. Coat the beef with the olive oil, paprika, salt and pepper.

2. To make the Lemon Yoghurt Dressing, mix all the ingredients in a small bowl. Chill until ready to serve.

3. Cook the beef on the barbecue or in a hot frying pan for 3–6 minutes on each side, until done to your liking. Transfer to a board to rest for 5 minutes, then thinly slice.

4. While the beef is resting, cut the pita pockets in half and heat on the barbecue or in a toaster.

5. Serve the warm pita pockets filled with sliced steak, tomatoes, feta, spinach and avocado, and drizzled with Lemon Yoghurt Dressing.

TIPS AND TRICKS
+ The pita pockets could be swapped out for regular or gluten-free wraps.
+ Add or swap in your favourite salad vegetables.

My Classic Pasta Salad

You will find a pasta salad at every Kiwi or Aussie barbecue because it's the perfect side dish to serve up with grilled meat. This one is my go-to with a super-easy home-made dressing. Topped with feta and eggs, it will be gone in no time!

500 g (1 lb 2 oz) bow-tie pasta
200 g (7 oz) cherry tomatoes, halved
75 g (2½ oz) feta, crumbled
½ cucumber, sliced
1 spring onion, finely sliced
4 hard-boiled eggs, peeled and cut into wedges

SMOKED PAPRIKA DRESSING
½ cup mayonnaise
½ cup sour cream
1 Tbsp Dijon mustard
1 Tbsp finely chopped fresh parsley
1 tsp lemon juice
½ tsp sugar
½ tsp salt
¼ tsp smoked paprika
¼ tsp cracked black pepper

1. Cook the pasta according to the packet instructions until al dente. Drain and return to the pot.

2. Add the tomatoes, feta, cucumber and spring onion, reserving a little of each for the garnish.

3. To make the Smoked Paprika Dressing, whisk all the ingredients in a small bowl. Add to the pasta and stir together.

4. Transfer to a serving dish and top with the boiled egg and reserved tomatoes, feta, cucumber and spring onion.

5. Serve while warm or chill until ready to serve.

TIPS AND TRICKS

+ *Pasta shapes that work well in this recipe include bow-ties, penne and spirals.*
+ *Tasty additions or substitutes include sun-dried tomatoes, olives, red or yellow capsicum, crispy bacon, cooked chicken, chorizo, corn, red onion, cooked asparagus or green beans, peas and even canned tuna.*

My Favourite Dressings and Sauces

I like to have a few easy dressings and sauces up
my sleeve, and these are my faves.

Orange and Honey Dressing

¼ cup olive oil
¼ cup orange juice
1 Tbsp wholegrain mustard
1 Tbsp apple cider vinegar
2 tsp honey
salt and cracked black pepper, to taste

Place all the ingredients in a small bowl or jug
and whisk together.

Satay Sauce

⅓ cup boiling water
¼ cup peanut butter
2 Tbsp soy sauce
1 Tbsp sweet chilli sauce
1 tsp brown sugar
½ tsp ground ginger

Place all the ingredients in a small bowl or jug
and whisk together.

Chipotle Mayo Dressing

½ cup thick mayonnaise
1½ Tbsp chipotle sauce
1 Tbsp lemon or lime juice
¼ tsp paprika
¼ tsp salt

Place all the ingredients in a small bowl or jug
and whisk together.

Asian Dressing

1 Tbsp apple cider vinegar
1 Tbsp honey
1 Tbsp soy sauce
1 Tbsp olive oil
½ tsp sesame oil

Place all the ingredients in a small bowl or jug
and whisk together.

Vietnamese Dressing

2 Tbsp soy sauce
1 Tbsp fish sauce
1 Tbsp rice wine vinegar
1 Tbsp brown sugar
1 clove garlic, crushed
1 tsp sesame oil
½ tsp crushed chilli

Place all the ingredients in a small bowl or jug and whisk together.

Marie Rose Dressing

½ cup thick mayonnaise
3 Tbsp tomato sauce
1 Tbsp lime juice
2 tsp Worcestershire sauce
½ tsp paprika

Place all the ingredients in a small bowl or jug and whisk together.

Miso Dressing

3 Tbsp rice bran oil
3 Tbsp soy sauce
2 Tbsp rice wine vinegar
1 Tbsp miso paste
1 Tbsp brown sugar
1 clove garlic, crushed
1 tsp sesame oil
½ tsp crushed chilli

Place all the ingredients in a small bowl or jug and whisk together.

Balsamic Dressing

2 Tbsp olive oil
1 tsp wholegrain mustard
1 tsp balsamic vinegar
1 tsp runny honey
1 tsp water
salt and cracked black pepper, to taste

Place all the ingredients in a small bowl or jug and whisk together.

Home-made Herby Garlic Mayo

½ cup chopped mixed fresh herbs, such as
parsley, sage, mint or basil
½ cup vegetable oil
1 egg
2 Tbsp lemon juice
1 clove garlic, crushed
1 tsp wholegrain mustard
½ tsp honey
¼ tsp salt

Place all the ingredients in a small bowl or jug
and blend with a stick blender until creamy.

Cashew Pesto

2 cups fresh basil
1 cup roasted cashews
⅓ cup olive oil
½ cup grated parmesan
2 cloves garlic, crushed
2 Tbsp water
salt and cracked black pepper, to taste

Place all the ingredients in a food processor
and blend to a smooth paste. Taste and adjust
seasonings. Transfer to an airtight jar or
container and chill until ready to serve.

Smoked Fish Dip

300 g (10½ oz) smoked fish (we use trout)
200 g (7 oz) cream cheese, softened
125 g (4½ oz) sour cream
1 spring onion, sliced
2 tsp finely grated lemon zest
¼ cup lemon juice
salt and cracked black pepper, to taste

Flake the fish in a mixer or by hand until
finely shredded. Add the cream cheese, sour
cream, spring onion, lemon zest and juice
and mix well until combined, scraping down
the sides of the bowl as needed. Taste and
adjust seasonings. Transfer to an airtight jar
or container and chill until ready to serve.

Creamy Pesto Dressing

3 Tbsp pesto
3 Tbsp mayonnaise
1 Tbsp olive oil
1 Tbsp lime juice
salt and cracked black pepper, to taste

Place all the ingredients in a small bowl or jug
and whisk together.

Everyday Dinners

What's in this Chapter

CHICKEN BURRITO BOWLS • **PAGE 48**

GRILLED LAMB AND HALOUMI WRAPS • **PAGE 50**

CREAMY TUSCAN CHICKEN • **PAGE 52**

ONE-POT MINCE AND PASTA • **PAGE 54**

STICKY LEMON CHICKEN • **PAGE 56**

ROASTED TOMATO PRAWN PASTA • **PAGE 58**

BAKED MEDITERRANEAN MEATBALLS AND RICE • **PAGE 60**

CRISPY CHICKEN BREAST ON CREAMY PASTA • **PAGE 62**

ZUCCHINI AND RICOTTA CANNELLONI • **PAGE 64**

**HAWKER ROLLS WITH
SHREDDED CHICKEN**
● **PAGE 66**

**BAKED CRISPY CHICKEN
DRUMSTICKS** ● **PAGE 68**

**CREAMY ITALIAN
SAUSAGE PASTA** ● **PAGE 70**

**EASY CHICKEN
CURRY** ● **PAGE 72**

**GRILLED MISO SALMON
ON RICE NOODLES**
● **PAGE 74**

**TERIYAKI BEEF
WITH EGG NOODLES**
● **PAGE 76**

**PRAWN STIR-FRY WITH
CRISPY NOODLES** ● **PAGE 78**

**CLASSIC FAMILY-FRIENDLY
BURGERS** ● **PAGE 80**

**EASY PIZZA DOUGH +
MY FAVOURITE PIZZA
TOPPINGS** ● **PAGES 82–84**

Chicken Burrito Bowls

We love these burrito bowls in our house — particularly the kids because I give them extra corn chips to dip into the chicken and bean mixture. It's a versatile midweek family meal that's ready in just 30 minutes. You can swap the chicken mince for beef or pork mince if you prefer, and swap out the vegetables for your family's favourites.

1 Tbsp olive oil
1 onion, diced
500 g (1 lb 2 oz) chicken mince
2 cloves garlic, crushed
400 g (14 oz) can crushed tomatoes
1 tsp paprika
1 tsp ground cumin
¼ tsp cayenne pepper (optional)
1 tsp salt
425 g (15 oz) can red kidney beans, rinsed and drained

TO SERVE

2 cups cooked brown rice
1 cup fresh or frozen corn kernels, cooked
2 tomatoes, diced
1 cup grated cheese
¼ iceberg lettuce, shredded
2 cups crushed corn chips
½ cup sour cream
1 tsp paprika
1 handful fresh coriander (optional)

1. Heat the oil in a large frying pan over a medium heat. Add the onion and sauté until soft.

2. Add the chicken mince and garlic and cook until browned, breaking up the mince with a wooden spoon as it cooks.

3. Stir in the tomatoes, spices and salt, then the beans. Simmer for a further 5 minutes until everything is cooked through.

4. Serve the hot mince mixture in bowls on top of the cooked rice with corn, tomatoes, cheese, lettuce and crushed corn chips.

5. Mix the sour cream with the paprika and dollop on top of each burrito bowl, then garnish with coriander (if using). Serve immediately.

TIPS AND TRICKS

+ Leftover chicken and bean mix can be frozen and used later for tacos, nachos, burritos or quesadillas.
+ If you like some spice, finish with a drizzle of hot sauce.

Kids' fave

Grilled Lamb and Haloumi Wraps

The lamb in these wraps can be grilled in a frying pan or if the weather is nice then use the barbecue to add a smoky flavour. You'll be surprised at how good the mixed spice is on the lamb, giving it a lovely Mediterranean flavour that goes well with the salty haloumi. The easy tzatziki sauce balances out the big flavours perfectly.

450 g (1 lb) lamb leg steaks
2 Tbsp olive oil
3 cloves garlic, crushed
2 tsp ground mixed spice
½ tsp salt
180 g (6½ oz) haloumi
4 wraps
50 g (1¾ oz) rocket
12 cherry tomatoes, quartered
1 spring onion, sliced
¼ red onion, finely sliced (optional)

TZATZIKI
1 cup Greek yoghurt
½ cucumber, diced
1 Tbsp lemon juice
1 handful fresh mint, finely chopped
salt and cracked black pepper, to taste

1. Place the lamb in a bowl, add the oil, garlic, mixed spice and salt and turn to coat. Marinate for at least 20 minutes (if possible).

2. To make the Tzatziki, mix all the ingredients and chill until ready to serve.

3. Cook the lamb in a hot frying pan or on the barbecue for 3–4 minutes on each side, then transfer to a board to rest.

4. Cut the haloumi into 1 cm (½ in) slices. Fry or barbecue for 2 minutes on each side until golden.

5. Carve the lamb into 2 cm (¾ in) slices.

6. Warm the wraps in the oven or toast for 30 seconds on each side in a dry frying pan or on the barbecue.

7. To assemble, spread the warm wraps with a generous dollop of the Tzatziki, then add the rocket, tomatoes, spring onion, red onion (if using), sliced lamb and grilled haloumi. Wrap up and serve immediately.

TIPS AND TRICKS
+ *These wraps would also be delicious with beef steaks or chicken thighs in place of the lamb.*

Creamy Tuscan Chicken

I guarantee you'll fall in love with the big flavours in this sauce: cream, parmesan, sun-dried tomatoes, and Italian herbs. The chicken cooks in the delicious thick sauce and comes out so nice and tender. Serve it with my classic focaccia from page 152 — it's perfect for mopping up the yummy sauce. A fresh green salad with a vinaigrette dressing balances out the meal nicely.

1 Tbsp olive oil

600 g (1 lb 5 oz) chicken thighs

¼ cup finely sliced sun-dried tomatoes

3 cloves garlic, crushed

1 Tbsp Italian herbs

1 cup chicken stock

1 cup baby spinach

½ cup cream

½ cup grated parmesan

1. Heat the oil in a large frying pan over a medium heat. Add the chicken and brown for a few minutes on each side.

2. Make a gap in the centre of the pan and add the sun-dried tomatoes, garlic and Italian herbs. Stir in the stock, scraping all the flavour from the base of the pan.

3. Add the spinach and stir everything together. Simmer over a low heat for 10 minutes, stirring occasionally, until the chicken is cooked through.

4. Add the cream and parmesan, and simmer, stirring, for a few minutes until the sauce starts to thicken.

5. Coat each piece of chicken in the creamy sauce and serve immediately.

TIPS AND TRICKS

+ *Cooking times will differ depending on whether you use boneless or bone-in chicken thighs in this recipe. Either will work, just make sure they are cooked through before serving. I like to cut through the thickest piece to check.*

+ *This recipe is also delicious served on top of cooked pasta.*

One-pot Mince and Pasta

This dish has become one of the most popular recipes on my website. Everyone loves a one-pot meal, and this one is great because the pasta cooks with the mince in the sauce. You may think the addition of milk in the sauce sounds a little bit weird but, trust me, it adds to the flavour and makes the sauce nice and creamy. Serve your delicious pasta with a fresh salad and crusty garlic bread for an easy meal that's ready in no time and is a winner with young kids.

1 Tbsp olive oil
500 g (1 lb 2 oz) beef mince
1 onion, diced
1 handful baby spinach (optional)
400 g (14 oz) can crushed tomatoes
1 Tbsp tomato paste
3 cloves garlic, crushed
1 Tbsp Italian herbs
½ tsp chilli flakes (optional)
2 cups beef stock
1 cup milk
2 cups dried pasta
½ cup grated cheese

1. Heat the oil in a large frying pan over a medium heat. Add the mince and cook until browned, breaking it up with a wooden spoon as it cooks.

2. Add the onion and spinach (if using), and cook until the onion is soft.

3. Add the tomatoes, tomato paste, garlic, Italian herbs and chilli flakes (if using) and mix together well.

4. Stir in the stock and milk, then the pasta.

5. Bring to a boil, then reduce the heat to medium. Keep stirring every few minutes until the liquid has all been absorbed and the pasta is cooked al dente.

6. Scatter the cheese over the mince, let it melt, then serve immediately.

TIPS AND TRICKS

+ *The beef mince could be swapped for chicken or lamb mince.*
+ *Any shape of pasta pieces could be used — spirals, bow-ties, elbows, penne are all great.*

Kids' fave

Sticky Lemon Chicken

This delicious, light version of the popular takeaway dish packs a punch when it comes to flavour. The crispy chicken is coated in a sticky and tangy lemon sauce. Serve it with white rice, brown rice or rice noodles and a side of Asian greens, such as pak choy, or your favourite seasonal or frozen vegetables.

---

600 g (1lb 5 oz) boneless chicken thighs or breasts
½ cup cornflour
1 egg
½ cup chicken stock
⅓ cup lemon juice
¼ cup soy sauce
2 Tbsp brown sugar
2 Tbsp honey
2 tsp crushed garlic
2 Tbsp vegetable oil
1 Tbsp cornflour mixed with ¼ cup cold water
1 spring onion, sliced
1 tsp sesame seeds
1 handful fresh coriander (optional)

1. Cut the chicken into bite-sized pieces and place in a large bowl. Add the ½ cup cornflour and toss to coat. Add the egg and mix to coat the chicken. Set aside while you make the lemon sauce.

2. Place the stock, lemon juice, soy sauce, sugar, honey and garlic in a bowl and whisk together.

3. Heat the oil in a large frying pan over a medium heat. Working in batches, add the chicken pieces and fry until crispy on both sides. Remove from the frying pan and set aside.

4. Wipe the excess oil out of the frying pan. Add the lemon sauce and simmer for 2 minutes.

5. Stir in the cornflour mixture. Once the sauce starts to thicken, add the crispy chicken and turn to coat in the sticky lemon sauce.

6. Sprinkle with spring onion, sesame seeds and coriander (if using). Serve immediately.

TIPS AND TRICKS

+ *When preparing the chicken, the egg doesn't need to be whisked, just crack it over and mix it through — it will all work out.*

+ *If you find the sauce too sour, use less lemon juice or add a tablespoon more of brown sugar.*

Roasted Tomato Prawn Pasta

I came up with this recipe one summer when I had an abundance of ripe tomatoes in my garden. The roasted tomatoes give the sauce a lovely depth of flavour and go so well with the garlic and chilli flakes. Simply blitz up the roasted ingredients in a food processor to make the sauce, pan-fry the prawns and stir them both through the cooked angel hair pasta. Quick, easy and packed full of flavour, this is my ideal summer meal.

500 g (1 lb 2 oz) tomatoes, halved

4 cloves garlic, halved

½ tsp chilli flakes (optional)

2 Tbsp olive oil, plus extra to serve

salt and cracked black pepper, to taste

1 cup fresh basil, plus extra to serve

400 g (14 oz) angel hair pasta

400 g (14 oz) raw prawns, thawed with tails removed

2 Tbsp grated parmesan, to serve

1. Preheat the oven to 180°C (350°F) fan bake.

2. Place the tomatoes and garlic in a baking dish lined with baking paper. Scatter with the chilli flakes (if using) and drizzle with the olive oil. Season well with salt and pepper, then roast for 30 minutes.

3. Transfer the roasted tomatoes and juices to a blender or food processor. Add the basil and pulse until it is all combined.

4. Cook the pasta according to the packet instructions until al dente. Drain and set aside.

5. Pan-fry the prawns in a large frying pan until pink and cooked through.

6. Add the roasted tomato sauce and cooked pasta to the prawns and stir it all together. Taste and adjust seasonings.

7. Serve immediately, topped with parmesan, extra basil and a drizzle of olive oil.

TIPS AND TRICKS

+ *The roasted tomato sauce freezes well if you want to double the recipe.*

+ *Leave out the prawns if you want the recipe to be vegetarian.*

Baked Mediterranean Meatballs and Rice

The genius of this meal is that the meatballs and rice cook together in the oven at the same time. You simply place all the ingredients in the dish then put it in the oven. I like to grill mine with a little bit of feta at the end, then serve topped with fresh tomatoes and yoghurt sauce. This is an awesome one-pot wonder, keeping your dishes to a minimum!

1 cup long-grain white rice
1½ cups water
1 cup beef, chicken or
   vegetable stock
2 tsp finely grated lemon
   zest
1 Tbsp lemon juice
1 tsp ground cumin
1 tsp ground coriander
1 tsp garlic powder
20 pre-made beef
   meatballs
55 g (2 oz) feta, crumbled
1 handful fresh parsley or
   mint, chopped
2 tomatoes, diced
1 spring onion, finely sliced

MINTY YOGHURT SAUCE
1 cup Greek yoghurt
½ cucumber, diced
1 Tbsp lemon juice
1 handful fresh mint, finely
   chopped

1. Preheat the oven to 180°C (350°F) fan bake.

2. Place the rice in the bottom of a large ovenproof dish.

3. Add the water, stock, lemon zest and juice, cumin, coriander and garlic powder. Mix together.

4. Arrange the meatballs on top, then cover tightly with a lid or tinfoil. Bake for 1 hour or until the rice is almost cooked and most of the liquid has reduced.

5. Scatter with the crumbled feta and bake for another 10–15 minutes uncovered, until the rice is cooked through.

6. To make the Minty Yoghurt Sauce, mix all the ingredients in a small bowl or jar. Chill until ready to serve.

7. Remove the meatballs and rice from the oven and scatter with the parsley or mint. Serve in bowls topped with the tomatoes, spring onion and Minty Yoghurt Sauce.

TIPS AND TRICKS
+ *You can use either store-bought or home-made meatballs for this recipe. You'll need about 400 g (14 oz).*

Crispy Chicken Breast on Creamy Pasta

Everyone loves a traditional chicken parmigiana, and this recipe is loosely based on that popular meal. The delicious, creamy pasta is easy to make, packed full of flavour and could easily be served as a stand-alone meal. However, when you add on the crispy chicken breasts, you take the dish to the next level!

500 g (1 lb 2 oz) spiral pasta
500 g (1 lb 2 oz) chicken breasts
salt and cracked black pepper, to taste
¼ cup plain flour
1 egg, whisked
1 cup panko crumbs
2 Tbsp olive oil
1 onion, finely diced
1 red capsicum, diced
2 Tbsp chopped sun-dried tomatoes
2 Tbsp tomato paste
2 cloves garlic, crushed
1 tsp dried mixed herbs
1 cup cream
½ cup grated parmesan
1 handful fresh basil

TIPS AND TRICKS

+ *Swap the pasta spirals for penne, spaghetti or any shape you prefer.*

1. Cook the pasta according to the packet instructions until al dente. Drain and set aside.

2. While the pasta is cooking, slice each chicken breast in half lengthways, place under a piece of baking paper and flatten with a rolling pin or meat mallet to make it an even thickness. Season well with salt and pepper.

3. Put the flour, egg and panko crumbs in 3 separate bowls, then dip the chicken pieces into each of them in that order. Transfer to a plate and set aside while you make the pasta sauce.

4. Heat 1 tablespoon of the oil in a large frying pan, then add the onion and capsicum and sauté until soft. Stir in the sun-dried tomatoes, tomato paste, garlic and herbs and cook for a few minutes more.

5. Stir in the cream, then the parmesan. Taste and adjust seasonings. Once the sauce starts to thicken up, add the cooked pasta and stir to coat.

6. To cook the chicken, heat the remaining 1 tablespoon of oil in a large frying pan and fry the chicken on each side until cooked through and golden. Transfer to a board and slice each piece into strips.

7. Divide the creamy pasta between 4 plates, top with sliced chicken, and scatter with basil to serve.

Kids' fave

Zucchini and Ricotta Cannelloni

This cannelloni is one of my favourite vegetarian dinners, and a great way to use up zucchini in the height of summer! The grated zucchini is fried off with garlic, then combined with lemon zest and ricotta to make a beautiful filling for the cannelloni. Roll up the lasagne sheets, top with crushed tomatoes and cheese, and bake until it's golden and sizzling. Serve it with a side salad and garlic bread and you've got an amazing meal.

---

1 Tbsp olive oil
1 onion, sliced
750 g (1 lb 10 oz) zucchini
3 cloves garlic, crushed
2 tsp finely grated lemon
  zest
200 g (7 oz) ricotta
¼ cup lemon juice
salt and cracked black
  pepper, to taste
400 g (14 oz) fresh lasagne
  sheets
400 g (14 oz) can crushed
  tomatoes
1 Tbsp Italian herbs
1 cup grated cheese

1. Preheat the oven to 180°C (350°F) fan bake.

2. Heat the oil in a large frying pan and sauté the onion until soft.

3. Grate the zucchini onto a clean tea towel, then gather up the edges and squeeze over a sink to remove the excess liquid.

4. Add the zucchini to the frying pan and cook, turning frequently, for about 5 minutes. Stir in the garlic and lemon zest, then fry for a few more minutes. Stir in the ricotta and lemon juice. Season well with salt and pepper.

5. Cut the lasagne sheets into 8 even pieces, divide the ricotta mix between them, and roll up lengthways into cannelloni.

6. Pour half the tomatoes into an ovenproof dish large enough to hold all the cannelloni in a single layer. Add half the Italian herbs, then stir together.

7. Arrange the cannelloni on top of the sauce, seam-side down. Spread the remaining tomatoes and Italian herbs over the cannelloni. Scatter with the cheese.

8. Bake for 30 minutes until golden and bubbling.

Hawker Rolls with Shredded Chicken

It's hard to beat a tasty hawker roll. Roti on its own is obviously delicious, but this recipe for Asian-style chicken takes it to the next level. Baking and shredding chicken breasts is super-easy and yet not many people know how to do it. Because the chicken bakes in the sauce, it never dries out and takes on a lot of flavour.

1 cup chicken stock
¼ cup soy sauce
3 Tbsp sweet chilli sauce
2 Tbsp cornflour
1 Tbsp brown sugar
1 tsp Chinese five spice
1 tsp crushed garlic
1 tsp crushed ginger
1 kg (2 lb 4 oz) chicken breasts

TO SERVE
8 small roti
1 bag pre-made coleslaw
½ cucumber, sliced
2 spring onions, finely sliced
1 red chilli, finely sliced (optional)
1 handful fresh coriander
Japanese mayonnaise

1. Preheat the oven to 180°C (350°F) fan bake.

2. Mix together the stock, soy sauce, sweet chilli sauce, cornflour, sugar, five spice, garlic and ginger in a large ovenproof dish.

3. Add the chicken and turn to coat in the sauce. Cover with a lid or tinfoil and bake for 30 minutes. Remove the lid, turn the chicken over and bake for another 30 minutes until it is cooked through and tender.

4. Shred the chicken with 2 forks and toss to coat in the sauce.

5. Turn the oven up to 210°C (410°F), then add the dish back to the oven for 5 minutes to infuse the flavours through the shredded chicken.

6. Toast the roti in a toaster or dry frying pan until crispy. Serve hot, stacked with shredded chicken, coleslaw, cucumber, spring onions, chilli (if using) and coriander, and topped with a drizzle of mayonnaise.

TIPS AND TRICKS
+ *Freeze any leftover pulled chicken in sealable bags or an airtight container for up to 3 months.*
+ *This meal can also be served in a bowl on top of rice.*

Baked Crispy Chicken Drumsticks

The genius in this recipe is the way the drumsticks are coated, with no need for triple dipping and gluggy fingers! Simply place them in a large container with the flour and spices, put the lid on and shake to coat. Crack the egg in and shake again before coating in the panko crumbs. Bake until golden and cooked through, then serve with a simple coleslaw and some wedges on the side for an easy midweek meal.

8 chicken drumsticks
1 Tbsp plain flour
1 tsp ground cumin
1 tsp paprika
1 tsp garlic powder
½ tsp salt
1 egg
1 cup panko crumbs

1. Preheat the oven to 190°C (375°F) fan bake.

2. Line a baking tray with baking paper.

3. Place the drumsticks in a large container, then sprinkle with flour, cumin, paprika, garlic powder and salt. Top with a lid and give the container a good shake to coat the chicken. This can be done in advance.

4. Add the egg and shake again until the drumsticks are coated in the egg.

5. Spread the panko crumbs on a plate and roll each drumstick in the crumbs to coat.

6. Arrange the drumsticks in a single layer on the lined baking tray. Bake for 45 minutes until cooked through and golden.

TIPS AND TRICKS

✝ *These chicken drumsticks can be eaten cold or hot the next day. To reheat, make sure they are piping hot all the way through.*

Kids' fave

Creamy Italian Sausage Pasta

This is the perfect meal to jazz up sausages. I like to use Italian or Toulouse sausages because they're full of flavour, but any type will do. The secret to the creamy sauce is the cream cheese, which slowly melts in the pan, then mixes with the grated parmesan to thicken up. Served with a fresh salad on the side, this incredibly easy meal is ready in under 30 minutes.

500 g (1 lb 2 oz) penne or rigatoni pasta
500 g (1 lb 2 oz) Italian or Toulouse sausages
200 g (7 oz) mushrooms, sliced
4 cloves garlic, crushed
1 Tbsp Italian herbs
1 cup chicken stock
200 g (7 oz) cream cheese
½ cup milk
½ cup grated parmesan, plus extra to serve
salt and cracked black pepper, to taste
1 handful fresh basil or Italian parsley, coarsely chopped

1. Cook the pasta according to the packet instructions until al dente. Drain and set aside.

2. While the pasta is cooking, squeeze the sausage meat out of the casings into a large frying pan. Use a wooden spoon to break it up into small pieces, then cook over a medium heat for 5 minutes until starting to brown. Add the sliced mushrooms and cook for a further 5 minutes.

3. Stir in the garlic and Italian herbs and fry for a few minutes.

4. Add the stock, cream cheese and milk, then cook, stirring, until the cream cheese has melted.

5. Stir in the parmesan and simmer until the sauce thickens up. Taste and adjust seasonings.

6. Add the cooked pasta to the sauce and stir together.

7. Sprinkle with the basil or parsley and extra parmesan, and serve immediately.

TIPS AND TRICKS

✝ *Add a teaspoon of crushed chilli at the same time as the garlic if you like a bit of spice in your pasta. I always have a jar of ready-crushed chilli in the fridge to make this easy.*

Easy Chicken Curry

This is a nice mild chicken curry, suitable for kids. If you want a bit of kick, add some crushed chilli or chilli flakes in with the spices at the start. Adding the green peas right at the end keeps them green and tender. Serve on steamed rice with roasted cashews and parsley or coriander (if you like it).

500 g (1 lb 2 oz) boneless
   chicken thighs
1 Tbsp olive oil
1 onion, finely diced
1 Tbsp crushed garlic
1 Tbsp crushed ginger
1 Tbsp mild curry powder
2 tsp garam masala
½ tsp sugar
½ tsp salt
1 cup chicken stock
400 ml (14 fl oz) can
   coconut cream
salt and cracked black
   pepper, to taste
1 cup frozen peas

TO SERVE
2 cups steamed white rice
½ cup roasted cashews
1 handful fresh parsley or
   coriander

1. Cut the chicken into bite-sized pieces.

2. Heat the oil in a large frying pan, add the onion and sauté for 3 minutes. Stir in the garlic and ginger, then cook for 1 minute.

3. Add the chicken and cook for 5 minutes until brown.

4. Sprinkle in the curry powder, garam masala, sugar and salt, then stir through the chicken mixture for 2 minutes until fragrant.

5. Stir in the stock, scraping all the flavour from the base of the pan. Add the coconut cream and stir together.

6. Reduce the heat and simmer for 5 minutes until the chicken is cooked through.

7. Taste and adjust seasonings. Add the frozen peas and cook for 2 minutes until they are cooked through.

8. Serve on rice, topped with roasted cashews and parsley or coriander.

TIPS AND TRICKS
+ *Chicken breasts can be used instead of chicken thighs.*
+ *Add extra vegetables of your choice, but you may have to simmer for longer.*

Kids'
fave

Grilled Miso Salmon on Rice Noodles

I love eating salmon, and my favourite way to prepare it is under the grill. It saves the house from getting smoky, which is often the case when cooking it in a frying pan. In this super-easy recipe you just coat the salmon in the miso dressing, grill it until cooked through, and serve it on rice noodles and pak choy, which are also cooked in the yummy miso sauce. A light Asian-style meal that's perfect for any night of the week.

100 g (3½ oz) dried flat rice noodles
3 Tbsp low-salt soy sauce
1½ Tbsp brown sugar
1 Tbsp miso paste
2 tsp crushed ginger
1 tsp sesame oil
½ tsp crushed chilli
600 g (1 lb 5 oz) fresh salmon, boneless
3 bunches pak choy
1 tsp olive oil
1 handful fresh coriander
4 lime or lemon wedges

TIPS AND TRICKS

+ *I like to keep jars of ready-crushed chilli and ginger in the fridge to make recipes like this even quicker.*

1. Preheat the oven to 210°C (410°F) fan grill.

2. Place the rice noodles in a bowl, cover with boiling water and allow to stand for 5 minutes until softened. Drain and set aside.

3. Whisk the soy sauce, sugar, miso paste, ginger, sesame oil and chilli in a small jug.

4. Slice the salmon into 4 pieces. Place in an ovenproof dish and drizzle with half of the soy marinade, brushing to cover any gaps.

5. Cook under the grill for 10–15 minutes until golden brown and cooked to your liking.

6. Wash and slice the pak choy. Heat the olive oil in a large frying pan over a high heat, add the pak choy and stir-fry for a few minutes until starting to wilt.

7. Add the cooked noodles and the remaining soy marinade to the pan and cook, stirring, until the noodles are coated in the marinade and heated through.

8. Divide the noodles and pak choy between 4 bowls, then place a piece of salmon on each. Serve immediately, garnished with coriander and a wedge of lime.

Teriyaki Beef with Egg Noodles

This meal is an adaptation of my popular recipe for teriyaki chicken. Young kids love this style of meal because all the ingredients are in separate portions. Plus, the noodles are great for slurping up! Load up your bowl with your favourite fresh or frozen vegetables — I like edamame beans and grated carrot for colour. An easy, nutritious meal that's ready in a flash.

350 g (12 oz) packet egg noodles
600 g (1 lb 5 oz) beef sirloin or rump steak
1 Tbsp vegetable oil

TERIYAKI SAUCE
½ cup low-salt soy sauce
¼ cup water
2 Tbsp apple cider vinegar
2 Tbsp brown sugar
1 Tbsp cornflour
2 cloves garlic, crushed
1 tsp sesame oil

TO SERVE
2 carrots, peeled and shredded
1 cup edamame beans, cooked
1 Tbsp sesame seeds
4 Tbsp Japanese mayonnaise
sliced fresh red chilli, to taste (optional)

1. To make the Teriyaki Sauce, place all the ingredients in a small bowl and whisk together.

2. Cook the noodles according to the packet instructions. Drain and set aside.

3. Slice the beef into 1 cm (½ in) strips. Flatten each strip with a rolling pin or the flat side of a meat mallet.

4. Heat the oil in a large frying pan over a high heat. When the oil is hot, add the beef strips and fry for about 4 minutes until brown on both sides.

5. Make a gap in the centre of the pan, add the Teriyaki Sauce and stir until it thickens up. Add the cooked noodles and toss to coat in the sauce. Simmer for 2 minutes.

6. Divide the beef and noodles between 4 bowls, top with the carrot, edamame beans, sesame seeds, mayonnaise and sliced chilli (if using), and serve immediately.

TIPS AND TRICKS
+ *Flattening the beef first makes it nice and tender, but this step is optional if you're in a hurry.*
+ *You could use diced beef instead of steak.*
+ *To cook edamame beans, cover with water in a glass jug and microwave for 3 minutes. Drain and they are ready to serve.*

Kids' fave

Prawn Stir-fry with Crispy Noodles

This is my go-to stir-fry sauce, which can be used in almost any type of stir-fry. In this recipe I've used it with prawns, edamame beans and fresh vegetables, which makes for such a lovely combination. I like to add the crispy noodles right at the end so they keep their crunch. It's an easy meal that can be on the table in no time.

1 tsp sesame oil
½ cauliflower, chopped
1 red capsicum, sliced
1 carrot, peeled and sliced
a splash of water
1 cup edamame beans, thawed
500 g (1 lb 2 oz) raw prawns, thawed with tails removed
1 spring onion, sliced
80 g (2¾ oz) crispy noodles
1 tsp sesame seeds

STIR-FRY SAUCE
¼ cup low-salt soy sauce
2 Tbsp sweet chilli sauce
1 Tbsp brown sugar
1 Tbsp sesame oil
1 Tbsp cornflour
1 tsp crushed garlic
1 tsp crushed ginger
½ cup water

1. To make the Stir-Fry Sauce, combine all the ingredients in a small jug.

2. Heat the sesame oil in a large frying pan over a medium heat. Add the cauliflower, capsicum, carrot and a splash of water and stir-fry for 3 minutes.

3. Add the edamame beans and stir-fry for 2 minutes. Make a gap in the centre of the pan, add the prawns and stir-fry until the prawns are pink and cooked through.

4. Add the Stir-Fry Sauce and stir together. Simmer, stirring, for 2–3 minutes until the sauce thickens and everything is hot and cooked through.

5. Stir in the spring onion and crispy noodles, sprinkle with sesame seeds and serve immediately.

TIPS AND TRICKS
+ *I like to keep jars of ready-crushed garlic and ginger in the fridge to make recipes like this even easier.*

Classic Family-friendly Burgers

Home-made burgers are a family-favourite dinner. This recipe is kid-friendly, and each person can add their favourite toppings depending on their preferences. I like to finely grate the onions for the patties so my kids can't pick out the pieces! In fact, they don't even notice them. Jazz up your burgers however you like, or even make smaller patties for cute kids' sliders.

---

500 g (1 lb 2 oz) beef mince
1 egg
1 small onion, grated
¼ cup breadcrumbs
2 Tbsp barbecue sauce
1 tsp dried mixed herbs
1 tsp crushed garlic
1 tsp salt

TO SERVE
4 burger buns
¼ cup tomato sauce
4 cheese slices
¼ iceberg lettuce
½ red onion, finely sliced (optional)
1 large tomato, sliced
2 gherkins, sliced
¼ cup mayonnaise

1. Mix the mince with all the remaining ingredients in a large bowl.

2. Divide into 4 even portions, then shape into large patties about 2 cm (¾ in) thick. Chill until ready to barbecue or pan-fry. This can be done earlier in the day.

3. Cook the patties for 4–5 minutes each side in a hot frying pan or on the barbecue.

4. Once the patties are cooked, place a slice of cheese on top of each one.

5. Cut the buns in half and grill or toast until warm. Load up with the tomato sauce, patties and cheese, lettuce, red onion (if using), tomato, gherkin and mayonnaise — or fill with your favourite salad ingredients and sauces.

Kids' fave

Easy Pizza Dough

This simple recipe for home-made pizza dough will impress your friends and family. Just add your favourite toppings! The dough is so versatile. It's my go-to pizza dough because it's so easy to make, it turns out perfectly every time and it tastes amazing. Once you've nailed this recipe you won't need to buy pizza bases ever again. This makes 5 bases so I freeze any extra, pre-rolled for later.

2 cups warm water
2 tsp honey or sugar
2 tsp active dry yeast
5 cups high-grade flour
3 Tbsp olive oil
1½ tsp salt

TIPS AND TRICKS

+ *To freeze pizza bases, roll each piece of dough to the desired size then place on a sheet of baking paper. Repeat, separating each base with baking paper. Wrap in cling film or place in a large sealable bag and freeze for up to 3 months.*

1. Place the warm water and honey or sugar in a large bowl or the bowl of a stand mixer and stir to dissolve.

2. Add the yeast, then stir again. Cover with a tea towel and allow to stand for 10 minutes.

3. Add the flour, olive oil and salt and stir together. Knead with a dough hook or by hand for 5 minutes until smooth and a little sticky.

4. Cover with a tea towel and allow to rise in a warm place for at least 30 minutes until doubled in size.

5. Turn the dough out onto a well-floured bench, roll into a log shape and cut into 5 pieces. Roll each piece into a ball and allow to rise for another 15 minutes.

6. When you are ready to make the pizza, preheat the oven to 220°C (425°F) and place a pizza stone in the oven to heat.

7. Roll out the dough on a well-floured bench or a sheet of baking paper. Add pizza sauce and your favourite toppings (see overleaf for some of mine).

8. Bake on the hot pizza stone for 15–20 minutes, or until the base is golden.

My Favourite Pizza Toppings

One of the best things about pizza is that it is so versatile. I love to have pizza parties where everyone can create their own pizza using their favourite toppings. Here are some delicious combinations to get you inspired once you've made your own dough (see previous recipe).

Cheesy Garlic Pizza

Cover the base with finely chopped fresh garlic, then top with lots of grated mozzarella, dried Italian herbs and fresh Italian parsley.

Smoked Salmon and Cream Cheese Pizza

Cover the base with pizza sauce, then top with smoked salmon, cream cheese, capers, lemon zest and grated mozzarella.

Smoked Chicken and Cranberry Pizza

Cover the base with pizza sauce, then top with smoked chicken, camembert, cranberry sauce, grated mozzarella and rocket.

Barbecue Pulled Pork Pizza

Cover the base with pizza sauce, then top with pulled pork (see page 102), red onion, capsicum, barbecue sauce and grated mozzarella.

Prosciutto and Mushroom Pizza

Cover the base with pizza sauce, then top with mushrooms, prosciutto, bocconcini, grated mozzarella and fresh basil.

Prawn and Chilli Pizza

Cover the base with pizza sauce, then top with prawns, sliced fresh chilli, chopped fresh garlic and grated mozzarella.

Winter Warmers

What's in this Chapter

OVEN-BAKED FIVE SPICE PORK BELLY • PAGE 90

SMOKED FISH POT PIES • PAGE 92

SLOW-COOKER ASIAN BEEF IN BAO BUNS • PAGE 94

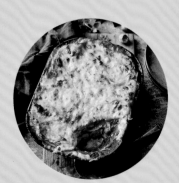

EPIC CHICKEN LASAGNE • PAGE 96

CHORIZO AND PEA OVEN-BAKED RISOTTO • PAGE 100

SLOW-COOKER BARBECUE PULLED PORK BURGERS • PAGE 102

Oven-baked Five Spice Pork Belly

I've been making this pork belly for years, and everyone who tries it is always impressed. Cooking it in the oven makes it extra tender, and then taking the lid off for the last 30 minutes crisps up the fat. Packed full of flavour and served on steamed rice with a side of pak choy, it's the perfect meal to make on the weekend when you have friends and family coming over. I guarantee they will be impressed!

1 kg (2 lb 4 oz) boneless pork belly strips, cut into bite-sized pieces
1 Tbsp plain flour
1 cup beef stock
1 cup boiling water

FIVE SPICE MARINADE
¼ cup soy sauce
2 Tbsp sweet chilli sauce
2 Tbsp apple cider vinegar
2 Tbsp brown sugar
2 tsp Chinese five spice
1 tsp ground coriander
1 tsp sesame oil
1 tsp garlic powder
a shake of chilli flakes
3 star anise (optional)
2 cinnamon sticks (optional)

TO SERVE
1 spring onion, sliced
1 Tbsp sesame seeds

1. Preheat the oven to 170°C (325°F) fan bake.

2. Place the pork in a baking dish, sprinkle with flour and turn to coat.

3. To make the Five Spice Marinade, combine all the ingredients in a jug. Pour the marinade over the pork and turn to coat. Add the stock, cover with a lid or tinfoil and bake for 1½–2 hours.

4. Remove from the oven, stir, then add the boiling water. Turn the oven up to 200°C (400°F) and bake uncovered for 30 minutes until the pork is looking and smelling amazing. If your sauce is too thick, add more water, or if it seems too thin, cook for a bit longer.

5. Scatter with the spring onion and sesame seeds to serve.

TIPS AND TRICKS

+ *If using star anise and cinnamon sticks, make sure you remove them before serving so people don't break their teeth.*
+ *To make this in a slow cooker, coat the pork pieces in flour, then pour in the marinade and stock. Stir well then cook on high for 3–4 hours, or on low for 7–8 hours, until the pork is tender and the sauce has thickened up. Transfer the pork to an ovenproof dish and grill it for 10 minutes to crisp it up at the end.*

Smoked Fish Pot Pies

My husband Mike loves fishing, and we often have smoked trout in our freezer. This is my favourite recipe to use it in! These individual pies look great when you serve them up, but you could easily make this in one large pie dish if you prefer.

1 onion, finely sliced
55 g (2 oz) butter
55 g (2 oz) plain flour
1 cup vegetable stock
1½ cups milk
2 Tbsp chopped fresh
 parsley
1 tsp wholegrain mustard
1 tsp finely grated lemon
 zest
¼ tsp freshly grated nutmeg
salt and cracked black
 pepper, to taste
200 g (7 oz) white fish or
 salmon, cut into cubes
200 g (7 oz) smoked fish,
 gently flaked
2 sheets puff pastry
1 egg, whisked

1. Preheat the oven to 180°C (350°F) fan bake.

2. In a large frying pan, sauté the onion with about a third of the butter for 5 minutes.

3. Add the remaining butter. When it is melted and bubbling, add the flour and stir for a minute to fry the mixture.

4. Add the stock half a cup at a time, stirring after each addition until there are no lumps. Add the milk half a cup at a time, stirring after each addition.

5. Add the parsley, mustard, lemon zest and nutmeg. Season to taste with salt and pepper.

6. Add both types of fish and gently stir through. Divide the mixture between 4 ramekins.

7. Cut rounds of puff pastry then place on top of the ramekins. Add any pastry decorations you like and brush with the egg wash.

8. Bake for 40 minutes until the pastry is flaky and golden. Allow to cool for 10–20 minutes before serving — the filling will be very hot.

TIPS AND TRICKS

+ *Boiled eggs, frozen peas or vegetables can be added at the same time as the fish.*
+ *These are also good topped with mashed potato instead of puff pastry.*

Slow-cooker Asian Beef in Bao Buns

We love bao buns in our house! I steam them until they're light and fluffy, then fill them with this delicious Asian-style sticky beef. Cooking the beef in the slow cooker makes it so tender, and the sauce thickens up towards the end so the beef becomes nice and sticky. Serve it with red cabbage, spring onions and cucumber to add a yummy crunch.

1 kg (2 lb 4 oz) beef
  casserole steak
1 onion, sliced
2 Tbsp plain flour

ASIAN MARINADE
1 cup beef stock
¼ cup soy sauce
¼ cup brown sugar
1 tsp Chinese five spice
1 tsp garlic powder
1 tsp ground ginger
1 tsp sesame oil

TO SERVE
12 bao buns, steamed
2 carrots, peeled and grated
  or julienned
¼ red cabbage, finely sliced
½ cucumber, finely sliced
2 spring onions, sliced
1 handful fresh coriander
Japanese mayonnaise

1. Place the beef and onion in a slow cooker, sprinkle with the flour, and stir to coat.

2. To make the Asian Marinade, combine all the ingredients in a small jug. Pour the marinade over the beef and onion, and stir to coat.

3. Cook on high for at least 4 hours, or on low for at least 6 hours, until the beef is tender.

4. Serve the sticky beef on steamed bao buns with carrots, cabbage, cucumber, spring onions, coriander and mayonnaise.

TIPS AND TRICKS
✛ Any leftovers can be stored in an airtight container in the freezer for up to 3 months. Reheat until piping hot.
✛ The plain flour can be swapped for gluten-free flour.

Epic Chicken Lasagne

I tried chicken lasagne for the first time when a friend made it in my teenage years and I've been dreaming about recreating it ever since. I think this one ticks all the boxes, and it's great served with crusty garlic bread and a fresh salad. I used to be scared of making a cheese sauce, but now that I've mastered it I would never use a bought sauce in a lasagne. It's so easy to make and really adds to the flavour. Once you've tried it you will be making it over and over!

1 Tbsp olive oil
1 onion, finely diced
1 carrot, peeled and finely diced
2 celery sticks, finely diced
1 Tbsp crushed garlic
600 g (1 lb 5 oz) chicken thighs, diced
2 Tbsp tomato paste
1 Tbsp Italian herbs
½ tsp sugar
400 g (14 oz) can crushed tomatoes
1 cup chicken stock
6 lasagne sheets
1 cup grated cheese

CHEESE SAUCE
55 g (2 oz) butter
55 g (2 oz) plain flour
2 cups milk
1 cup grated cheese
1 tsp wholegrain mustard
¼ tsp freshly grated nutmeg
salt and cracked black pepper, to taste

1. Preheat the oven to 180°C (350°F) fan bake.

2. Heat the oil in a large frying pan over a medium heat. Add the onion, carrot and celery and cook, stirring, for about 5 minutes.

3. Stir in the garlic, then add the chicken and cook, stirring, for a few minutes.

4. Stir in the tomato paste, Italian herbs and sugar. Stir in the tomatoes and stock, then simmer for 10 minutes until the liquid has reduced and the sauce has thickened up. Taste and adjust seasonings.

5. To make the Cheese Sauce, melt the butter in a large pot over a low heat. Add the flour and stir for a minute to fry the mixture. Add the milk a little at a time, stirring between each addition. Simmer gently until thick. Remove from the heat and stir in the cheese, mustard and nutmeg. Season well with salt and pepper.

6. Grease a large baking dish with oil. Cover the base of the dish with half of the chicken mixture then top with half of the lasagne sheets. Pour over half of the cheese sauce and spread to the edges.

CONTINUED OVERLEAF . . .

Kids' fave

7. Repeat with the remaining chicken mixture, lasagne sheets and cheese sauce, then scatter the top with the cheese.

8. Bake for 50 minutes until golden and bubbling. Remove from the oven and allow to stand for 15 minutes before serving.

TIPS AND TRICKS

+ *Any leftovers can be stored in an airtight container in the freezer for up to 3 months. Reheat until piping hot.*
+ *The recipe can be easily doubled if you want to make an extra lasagne and store it in the freezer.*
+ *This can be made using gluten-free lasagne sheets and gluten-free flour.*

Chorizo and Pea Oven-baked Risotto

I love to make baked risotto because the oven does all the work for you, so you don't need to stand at the stovetop stirring. Adding in the butter and parmesan at the end adds a depth of flavour, and the freshness of the peas goes so well with that spicy chorizo.

---

1 Tbsp olive oil
1 onion, diced
200 g (7 oz) chorizo, diced
3 cloves garlic, crushed
1½ cups arborio rice
4 cups chicken stock
1 cup frozen peas, thawed
½ cup grated parmesan,
   plus extra to serve
2 Tbsp butter
salt and cracked black
   pepper, to taste
2 Tbsp lemon juice
1 handful fresh basil or
   rocket, chopped

1. Preheat the oven to 180°C (350°F) fan bake.

2. Heat the oil in an ovenproof dish on the stovetop. Add the onion and sauté for a few minutes until soft.

3. Add the chorizo and garlic and cook, stirring, until the chorizo has browned.

4. Stir in the rice, and then slowly add the stock, stirring continuously.

5. Cover and bake for 35 minutes, stirring once halfway through cooking.

6. Remove from the oven, then add the peas, parmesan and butter. Gently fold together until the butter has melted. Taste and adjust seasonings.

7. Drizzle with lemon juice and scatter with basil or rocket and extra parmesan.

TIPS AND TRICKS

+ *The chorizo could be swapped for bacon or ham if you prefer.*
+ *Baked risottos are very versatile. Feel free to use this recipe as a guide and add your favourite ingredients.*

Slow-cooker Barbecue Pulled Pork Burgers

This is such a simple recipe and perfect if you're entertaining because you can throw all the ingredients into the slow cooker and let it simmer all day. I like to prep all the toppings and then let people serve themselves. The recipe makes enough pulled pork for 10 people so you can freeze half for a quick dinner another night. Alternatively, if you're cooking for a crowd, increase the buns and trimmings to suit.

1 onion, finely sliced

400 g (14 oz) can crushed tomatoes

¼ cup water

¼ cup barbecue sauce

2 Tbsp hickory sauce (optional)

2 Tbsp brown sugar

2 tsp crushed garlic

1 tsp salt

2½ kg (5 lb 8 oz) pork leg

2 Tbsp cornflour mixed with 2 Tbsp cold water

TO SERVE

4 burger buns, toasted

¼ iceberg lettuce

4 cheese slices

1 large tomato, sliced

¼ cup mayonnaise

¼ cup tomato relish (optional)

1. Place the onion, tomatoes and water in a slow cooker. Add the barbecue sauce, hickory sauce (if using), sugar, garlic and salt, and stir together.

2. Pat the pork dry, add to the slow cooker and turn to coat in the sauce. Cook on high for at least 5 hours, or low for at least 8 hours, until the pork is tender and falling apart.

3. Lift the pork out of the sauce and set aside. Stir the cornflour mixture into the sauce.

4. Shred the pork, discarding the skin and any bones, then stir it back into the sauce. Turn the slow cooker to warm until ready to serve.

5. Cut the buns in half and grill or toast until warm. Serve loaded with lettuce, pulled pork, cheese, tomato and mayonnaise. Add tomato relish, if desired.

TIPS AND TRICKS

+ *I spray my slow cooker with an oil spray before placing the meat in. This makes it easier to clean at the end.*
+ *Any leftovers can be stored in sealable bags or an airtight container in the freezer for up to 3 months. Reheat until piping hot and use on wraps, baked potatoes and pizzas.*

Kids' fave

Slow-cooker Moroccan Lamb with Couscous

Packed full of Moroccan flavours, this lamb is delicious served on couscous with a dollop of yoghurt. This is a double recipe, so you can freeze the other half of the lamb for another day. It's good with rice or jacket potatoes or as a pie filling in pastry or filo.

1 kg (2 lb 4 oz) lamb steaks, chops or shanks
1 onion, sliced
1 carrot, peeled and chopped
400 g (14 oz) can chickpeas, rinsed and drained
400 g (14 oz) can crushed tomatoes
1 cup natural yoghurt
½ cup dried apricots, chopped
2 Tbsp plain flour
1 cup beef stock
1 tsp ground cumin
1 tsp ground coriander
1 tsp ground ginger
1 tsp ground cinnamon
1 tsp ground turmeric
1 tsp brown sugar
1 tsp salt

TO SERVE
2 cups cooked couscous
2 Tbsp chopped fresh Italian parsley
¼ cup Greek yoghurt

1. Place the lamb, onion, carrot, chickpeas, tomatoes, yoghurt, apricots and flour in a slow cooker.

2. Whisk the stock, cumin, coriander, ginger, cinnamon, turmeric, sugar and salt in a bowl or jug. Add to the slow cooker and stir together.

3. Cook on high for at least 4 hours, or low for at least 6 hours, until the lamb is tender and falling apart. Taste and adjust seasonings.

4. Serve on fluffy couscous, garnished with parsley and a dollop of yoghurt.

TIPS AND TRICKS

+ *You can freeze the leftovers in an airtight container or sealable bag for up to 3 months.*
+ *If you use chops that are quite fatty, spoon off and discard the extra fat that has risen to the top before serving.*
+ *If you're missing any of the spices don't worry — it will still have great flavour.*
+ *To make this in the oven, combine all the ingredients in a large casserole dish, cover and cook for 2 hours at 170°C (325°F) fan bake. Remove the lid and cook for a further 30 minutes until it smells amazing and the meat is falling off the bone.*

Easy Cheesy Potato Bake

This recipe has only four ingredients, not counting the seasonings. You can use either cream or milk, depending on what you have or how healthy you want to be, but I make a half-and-half mixture using both milk and cream. The trick is to cook it for a long time until the potatoes are tender and golden on top. Make sure you use fresh garlic as this adds a subtle flavour to the creamy potatoes. Serve it as a side dish with any warming winter meals.

1 kg (2 lb 4 oz) potatoes, peeled
1½ cups cream and/or milk
2 cloves garlic, crushed
salt and cracked black pepper, to taste
1 cup grated cheese

1. Preheat the oven to 190°C (375°F) fan bake.

2. Thinly slice the potatoes.

3. Mix the cream and/or milk and garlic, and season well with salt and pepper.

4. Arrange a thin layer of potatoes in the base of an ovenproof dish. Sprinkle with cheese then pour over some of the creamy mixture.

5. Repeat these layers, using all of the potatoes, creamy mixture and cheese.

6. Bake for 1 hour 20 minutes until the potatoes are cooked through and the top is golden.

TIPS AND TRICKS

+ *You can use your favourite type of cheese in this dish. I use Colby, which melts well.*

Epic Big-batch Chilli Con Carne

This easy recipe will become your go-to for chilli con carne. It makes a huge batch of mince and beans, so you can freeze half for later or serve it at a large family meal.

1 Tbsp olive oil

1 onion, finely diced

1 red capsicum, finely diced

1 kg (2 lb 4 oz) lean beef mince

1½ Tbsp ground cumin

1½ Tbsp paprika

1½ Tbsp garlic powder

400 g (14 oz) can red kidney beans, drained and rinsed

400 g (14 oz) can black beans, drained and rinsed

400 g (14 oz) can crushed tomatoes

3 Tbsp tomato paste

3 Tbsp chipotle sauce

1 tsp salt

1 beef stock cube

1½ cups boiling water

TO SERVE

2 cups cooked white rice

1 cup grated cheese

½ cup sour cream

flesh of 1 avocado, diced

100 g (3½ oz) corn chips

1. Heat the oil in a large frying pan over a medium heat. Add the onion and capsicum and sauté until soft.

2. Add the mince, cumin, paprika and garlic powder and cook for about 5 minutes until browned, breaking up the mince with a wooden spoon as it cooks.

3. Add the kidney beans, black beans, crushed tomatoes, tomato paste, chipotle sauce and salt. Dissolve the stock cube in the boiling water and pour into the frying pan.

4. Mix everything together, then reduce the heat to low. Simmer for 30–40 minutes with the lid on, stirring every 10 minutes or so. Taste and adjust seasonings.

5. Serve on rice, topped with cheese, sour cream and avocado, with corn chips on the side.

TIPS AND TRICKS

+ *If you like your chilli hot, add some cayenne pepper or chilli flakes at the same time as the spices. If you prefer it mild, leave out the chipotle sauce.*

+ *The leftover mince mixture can be stored in an airtight container in the freezer for up to 3 months. Reheat until piping hot before serving. Chilli con carne is very versatile and can be served on rice, wrapped in a tortilla, as a burrito or with nacho chips.*

Kids' fave

Cauliflower Cheese and Gnocchi Bake

We love cauliflower cheese in our house and in this recipe I've put my own unique spin on it. Part pasta bake, part cauliflower cheese, it's a great vegetarian option that can be served as a main meal or side dish. You can swap the gnocchi out for cooked pasta if you prefer, or add chopped chicken for extra protein. It's the ultimate in easy comfort food, especially in the cooler months.

½ cauliflower, cut into florets
500 g (1 lb 2 oz) gnocchi
55 g (2 oz) butter
55 g (2 oz) plain flour
2 cups milk
1 cup grated cheese
1 tsp wholegrain mustard
salt and cracked black pepper, to taste
2 spring onions, finely sliced
1 handful fresh parsley, chopped
200 g (7 oz) cherry tomatoes
½ cup grated parmesan

1. Preheat the oven to 200°C (400°F) fan bake.

2. Bring a large pot of water to a boil, add the cauliflower and cook for 5 minutes until just cooked. Add the gnocchi and cook for 1 more minute. Drain and set aside while you make the sauce.

3. Melt the butter in a large pot over a low heat. Add the flour and stir for a minute to fry the mixture. Add the milk a little at a time, stirring between each addition. Simmer gently until thick.

4. Remove from the heat and stir in the cheese and mustard. Season well with salt and pepper.

5. Stir in the spring onions and parsley, then the cooked cauliflower and gnocchi.

6. Add the cherry tomatoes and gently stir together.

7. Transfer to a baking dish, top with parmesan and bake for 25 minutes until golden and bubbling.

TIPS AND TRICKS

+ *I use vacuum-sealed packets of gnocchi, which can be found in the pasta section of the supermarket.*

Hearty Beef, Mushroom and Potato Stew

This hearty beef stew reminds me of an old-style Irish stew. It's my dad's favourite and he asks for it every time he comes to visit. The potatoes bake in the delicious gravy, which makes for a tasty and comforting winter meal.

1 kg (2 lb 4 oz) diced casserole beef
2 Tbsp plain flour
1 tsp salt
½ tsp cracked black pepper
2 Tbsp olive oil
500 g (1 lb 2 oz) small potatoes, halved
250 g (9 oz) mushrooms, quartered
1 large onion, sliced into wedges
3 carrots, peeled and cut into chunks
3 celery sticks, sliced
2 cups beef stock
1 cup water
2 Tbsp Worcestershire sauce
1 tsp crushed garlic
2 Tbsp cornflour mixed with 2 Tbsp cold water
1 handful fresh parsley, chopped, to serve

1. Preheat the oven to 170°C (325°F) fan bake.

2. Place the diced beef in a bowl. Add the flour, salt and pepper, and mix to coat.

3. Heat the oil in a large casserole dish over a high heat. Working in batches, add the beef and fry for a few minutes on each side until browned.

4. Return all the beef and any cooking juices to the casserole dish and remove from the heat. Add all the remaining ingredients except the cornflour mixture and parsley. Cover with the lid or tinfoil and bake for 1½ hours.

5. Remove from the oven, add the cornflour mixture and stir together. Bake uncovered for a further 30 minutes until the sauce has thickened up and the meat is tender.

6. Scatter with the parsley and serve with steamed greens, if desired.

TIPS AND TRICKS

+ *Browning the meat first is not essential, but does add an extra depth of flavour.*
+ *You could serve this on mash as shown in the photo, but it is hearty enough to serve on its own.*
+ *The plain flour can be swapped for gluten-free flour.*
+ *This makes a large batch, so you can freeze extra portions in an airtight container for up to 3 months.*

Whole Roasted Pumpkin Soup

People are so surprised when I let them know you can cook a whole pumpkin in the oven. It saves you chopping, and the flesh of the pumpkin becomes lovely and tender. I like to roast the onion at the same time so it gets caramelised, then you simply need to fry it off, add the pumpkin and stock and blitz it all together. Serve with crusty croutons and a shaving of parmesan for a hearty winter soup. It also freezes well for later.

1 butternut pumpkin
1 onion
2 Tbsp olive oil
4 cloves garlic, crushed
1 tsp ground cumin
3 cups vegetable stock
salt and cracked black
　pepper, to taste

CROUTONS
½ loaf crusty white bread
1 Tbsp olive oil

TO SERVE
2 Tbsp grated parmesan
1 Tbsp chopped fresh Italian
　parsley
4 tsp cream (optional)

1. Preheat the oven to 170°C (325°F) fan bake.

2. Line an oven tray with baking paper.

3. Place the whole pumpkin on the lined oven tray. Cut the ends off the onion and cut the unpeeled onion in half. Drizzle with 1 tablespoon of the olive oil and place on the tray skin-side down.

4. Bake for 1 hour 40 minutes or up to 2 hours, depending on the size of your pumpkin. It is cooked when the skin has browned and it is easily pierced with a fork.

5. To make the Croutons, tear the bread into bite-sized chunks and spread out on an oven tray. Drizzle with olive oil, then bake for about 15 minutes until golden.

6. Once the pumpkin has cooled, peel off and discard the skin. Cut the pumpkin in half and scoop out and discard the seeds. Chop the flesh into large pieces or mash it. Discard the onion skin and coarsely chop the onion.

7. To make the soup, heat the remaining 1 tablespoon olive oil in a large pot, add the garlic and sauté for 1 minute.

CONTINUED OVERLEAF . . .

8. Add the onion and cumin to the pot and stir together.

9. Stir in the pumpkin and stock, bring to a simmer and cook for 5–10 minutes.

10. Remove from the heat and use a stick blender to purée the soup. Taste and adjust seasonings.

11. Serve topped with the home-made croutons, parmesan, parsley and a swirl of cream (if using).

TIPS AND TRICKS

+ *If you don't have a stick blender, you can roughly mash the soup with a potato masher or wait for it to cool and transfer it to a blender to get it smooth.*

+ *Any leftovers can be stored in an airtight container in the freezer for up to 3 months. Reheat until piping hot.*

Home Baking

What's in this Chapter

GINGERBREAD LOAF • PAGE 122

VANILLA SPRINKLE CAKE • PAGE 124

LEMON BUNDT CAKE • PAGE 126

RASPBERRY, COCONUT AND WHITE CHOCOLATE MUFFINS • PAGE 128

CLASSIC CHOCOLATE CAKE WITH BUTTERCREAM FROSTING • PAGE 130

BANANA MUFFINS WITH LEMON ICING • PAGE 134

BAKED LEMON SLICE • PAGE 136

ORANGE AND CHOCOLATE CHIP LOAF • PAGE 138

TROPICAL PINEAPPLE CAKE WITH CREAM CHEESE ICING • PAGE 140

Gingerbread Loaf

This is hands-down the best gingerbread loaf you'll ever make. Perfectly moist, it's a great treat for morning tea and I also love to serve it toasted the next day. Simply put a couple of pieces in the toaster until nice and golden, spread with a generous amount of butter and enjoy an indulgent breakfast.

150 g (5½ oz) butter

100 ml (3½ fl oz) golden syrup

2 cups plain flour

1 cup brown sugar, plus 1 Tbsp extra for topping

1 Tbsp ground ginger

1 tsp baking powder

1 tsp baking soda

1 tsp ground cinnamon

½ tsp salt

1 egg

1 cup milk

1. Preheat the oven to 170°C (325°F) fan bake.

2. Line a 27 x 13 cm (10¾ x 5 in) loaf tin with baking paper.

3. Melt the butter and golden syrup in a glass jug in the microwave, then stir together.

4. Place the flour, sugar, ginger, baking powder, baking soda, cinnamon and salt in a large bowl and whisk together.

5. Make a well in the centre, add the butter and golden syrup mixture, the egg and the milk and stir together.

6. Transfer to the lined loaf tin and scatter the extra tablespoon of brown sugar over the top.

7. Bake for 1 hour, or until a skewer inserted into the centre comes out clean.

8. Store in an airtight container in the pantry for up to 5 days.

Vanilla Sprinkle Cake

This cake is pure joy to look at, plus it tastes delicious. Because of its size and fun colours, it's a great option for children's birthday parties, shared morning teas, kindy celebrations or just to brighten up school lunches. I love cakes made in a big tin like this because they feed a crowd and are easier to slice up than round cakes!

2 cups plain flour
2 tsp baking powder
1 cup white sugar
125 g (4½ oz) butter
½ cup milk
2 tsp vanilla essence
2 eggs, whisked
2 Tbsp sprinkles

VANILLA ICING
80 g (2¾ oz) butter, softened
1½ cups icing sugar
1 tsp vanilla essence
2 Tbsp milk

1. Preheat the oven to 170°C (325°F) fan bake.

2. Line a 30 x 22 cm (12 x 8½ in) cake tin with baking paper.

3. Whisk together the flour, baking powder and sugar in a large bowl.

4. Melt the butter in a glass jug in the microwave. Stir in the milk and vanilla, then add to the dry ingredients with the eggs and stir together.

5. Gently fold in half the sprinkles and mix until all ingredients are just combined.

6. Transfer to the lined cake tin and bake for 30 minutes, or until a skewer inserted into the centre comes out clean.

7. Allow to cool in the tin for 10 minutes before transferring to a wire rack.

8. To make the Vanilla Icing, whip the butter in a stand mixer or with hand-held beaters on high for 1 minute. Add the icing sugar, vanilla and milk, and beat until smooth, pale and fluffy.

9. Spread the icing over the cooled cake and scatter with the remaining sprinkles to serve.

10. Store in an airtight container in the pantry for up to 4 days.

Kids' fave

Lemon Bundt Cake

If you have a lemon tree, this is the recipe for you! This soft and fluffy lemon cake topped with a tangy lemon glaze makes a lovely morning tea. I love the way the icing drips down the ridges from the bundt tin.

150 g (5½ oz) butter, softened
1 cup white sugar
2 eggs
½ cup Greek yoghurt
3 Tbsp finely grated lemon zest
½ cup lemon juice
2 cups plain flour
1 tsp baking powder
1 tsp baking soda

LEMON GLAZE
1½ cups icing sugar
2 Tbsp boiling water
1 Tbsp finely grated lemon zest
2 Tbsp lemon juice

1. Preheat the oven to 170°C (325°F) fan bake.

2. Grease and flour a 29 x 9 cm (11½ x 3½ in) bundt tin.

3. Cream the butter and sugar together in a stand mixer or with hand-held beaters until light and fluffy. Add the eggs and mix again. Add the yoghurt and lemon zest and juice and mix together.

4. Sift in the flour, baking powder and soda, and stir together until just combined.

5. Transfer to the prepared bundt tin and bake for 40–45 minutes, or until a skewer inserted into the centre comes out clean.

6. Allow to cool in the tin before turning out onto a serving plate.

7. To make the Lemon Glaze, whisk together the icing sugar, boiling water and lemon zest and juice.

8. Drizzle the glaze over the cooled cake to serve.

9. Store in an airtight container in the pantry for up to 3 days.

TIPS AND TRICKS

+ If you don't have a bundt tin, this cake can be made in a round tin or loaf tin (note that cooking time may vary).
+ Grease the tin with either cooking spray or butter, then place a tablespoon of flour in the bottom. Bang and shake the tin around until the flour has covered every surface.
+ If your glaze is too thick to drizzle, add a little more boiling water. If it's too thin, add a little more icing sugar.

Raspberry, Coconut and White Chocolate Muffins

It's always good to have a simple muffin recipe up your sleeve and these will not disappoint. The recipe is very versatile, so you can swap out the raspberries or white chocolate for whatever berries or chocolate you have on hand, and leave out the coconut if you don't like it. They can easily be frozen and they're perfect for school lunches.

1 cup white sugar
1 cup milk
½ cup vegetable oil
100 g (3½ oz) butter, melted
2 eggs
1 tsp vanilla essence
2½ cups plain flour
1 Tbsp baking powder
½ cup desiccated coconut
1 cup white chocolate chips
1 cup frozen (or fresh) raspberries
1 Tbsp brown sugar, to dust

1. Preheat the oven to 190°C (375°F) fan bake.

2. Arrange 12 paper cases in a muffin tin or tins.

3. Whisk the white sugar, milk, oil, butter, eggs and vanilla together in a large bowl.

4. Sift in the flour and baking powder. Add the coconut and gently fold the mixture together. Add the white chocolate chips and raspberries and stir until just combined.

5. Divide the mixture between the paper cases and sprinkle the brown sugar over the top.

6. Bake for 20–25 minutes until cooked through and golden on top. Allow to cool for a few minutes before transferring to a wire rack.

7. Store in an airtight container in the pantry for up to 4 days.

TIPS AND TRICKS

+ *These are best frozen on the day they are made. Cool completely and then place in a sealable bag or wrap in cling film or tinfoil. Freeze for up to 1 month. Thaw in the fridge overnight or pop a frozen muffin into a lunchbox — it will thaw by lunchtime.*

Kids' fave

Classic Chocolate Cake with Buttercream Frosting

This is my absolute go-to chocolate cake, ideal for a child's birthday cake. The whole cake is made in the mixer, keeping the dishes to a minimum and your hands free to keep working! The cake itself is not too sweet, which balances out the sweet raspberry buttercream. I've added a chocolate buttercream recipe as a tip, so you can choose your preference. The chocolate sprinkle topping is great for birthday parties, while the freeze-dried raspberry version is slightly more sophisticated.

150 g (5½ oz) butter, melted
1½ cups white sugar
2 eggs
1 tsp vanilla essence
½ cup milk
2 cups plain flour
½ cup cocoa powder
1 tsp baking powder
¼ tsp salt
1 tsp baking soda
1 tsp instant coffee
1 cup boiling water

RASPBERRY BUTTERCREAM
100 g (3½ oz) butter, softened
30 g (1 oz) frozen raspberries, thawed
1½ cups icing sugar
1 Tbsp crushed freeze-dried raspberries

1. Preheat the oven to 170°C (325°F) fan bake.

2. Line a 22 cm (8½ in) square cake tin with baking paper.

3. Place the butter, sugar, eggs and vanilla in the bowl of a stand mixer and whisk together at medium speed. Add the milk and whisk again.

4. Sift in the flour, cocoa, baking powder and salt.

5. Dissolve the baking soda and coffee in the boiling water, add to the bowl and whisk at medium speed until there are no lumps.

6. Transfer to the lined cake tin and bake for 50–60 minutes, or until a skewer inserted into the centre comes out clean.

7. Allow to cool in the tin for 20 minutes before transferring to a wire rack.

CONTINUED OVERLEAF . . .

8. If making Raspberry Buttercream, whip the butter in a stand mixer or with hand-held beaters for 2 minutes until pale. Mash the thawed raspberries with the back of a spoon, then add to the butter along with the icing sugar. Whip on a high speed until light and fluffy, scraping down the sides of the bowl as needed.

9. Spread the buttercream over the cooled cake and scatter with the freeze-dried raspberries.

TIPS AND TRICKS

+ *This could also be made in a round cake tin (note that cooking time may vary).*
+ *The instant coffee brings out the chocolate flavour, but you can leave it out if you prefer.*
+ *To make Chocolate Buttercream instead, whip 100 g (3½ oz) softened butter in a stand mixer or with hand-held beaters for 2 minutes until pale. Add 1½ cups icing sugar, 3 Tbsp cocoa and 2 Tbsp milk. Whip on a high speed until light and fluffy, scraping down the sides of the bowl as needed. Decorate with sprinkles.*

Banana Muffins with Lemon Icing

These cute banana muffins are delicious with or without the lemon icing. My grandma Bonnie used to make them for my siblings and me and we absolutely loved them. Baking them reminds me of her and proves that classic recipes like this are popular for a reason. The recipe makes 18 standard-sized muffins or at least 24 mini ones.

100 g (3½ oz) butter
1 cup white sugar
2 eggs
1 tsp vanilla essence
2 bananas, mashed
¾ cup milk
2 cups plain flour
1 tsp baking powder
1 tsp baking soda

LEMON ICING
2 cups icing sugar
2 Tbsp butter, softened
1 Tbsp finely grated lemon
  zest, plus extra to garnish
2 Tbsp lemon juice
1 Tbsp boiling water

1. Preheat the oven to 170°C (325°F) fan bake.

2. Arrange 18 paper cases in muffin tins.

3. Melt the butter in a large glass bowl in the microwave. Stir in the sugar, eggs and vanilla, then the bananas and milk.

4. Sift in the flour, baking powder and soda and fold together until combined. Divide the mixture evenly between the paper cases.

5. Bake for 18–23 minutes until cooked through and golden on top.

6. Allow to cool for a few minutes before transferring the muffins (still in their paper cases) to a wire rack.

7. To make the Lemon Icing, mix the icing sugar, butter, lemon zest and juice. Add the boiling water and whisk until there are no lumps.

8. Spread the icing over the cooled muffins with a butter knife, and garnish with extra lemon zest.

9. Store in an airtight container in the pantry for up to 4 days.

TIPS AND TRICKS
+ *You could add chocolate chips if you like.*

Kids' fave

Baked Lemon Slice

I love lemon slice, and this one has a base that's almost like shortbread, topped with tangy lemon custard and baked until it's perfectly set. Once it has chilled and set, slice it into squares and sprinkle with icing sugar to serve.

---

150 g (5½ oz) butter
¼ cup caster sugar
2 tsp finely grated lemon zest
1½ cups plain flour
1 tsp baking powder

LEMON TOPPING
4 eggs
¾ cup caster sugar
4 tsp finely grated lemon zest
¼ cup plain flour
1 tsp baking powder
100 ml (3½ fl oz) lemon juice

TO SERVE
1 Tbsp icing sugar, to dust

TIPS AND TRICKS
+ *Freeze lemon juice and zest in ice-cube trays while lemons are in season, then you can make this slice at any time of the year.*

1. Preheat the oven to 170°C (325°F) fan bake.

2. Line a 27 x 17 cm (10½ x 6½ in) slice tin with baking paper.

3. Melt the butter in a large glass bowl in the microwave. Add the sugar and lemon zest and whisk together.

4. Sift in the flour and baking powder, then mix until combined.

5. Transfer to the lined slice tin and press out evenly, smoothing the top with the back of a metal spoon.

6. Bake for 15 minutes until starting to brown. Allow to cool for 5 minutes before adding the topping.

7. To make the Lemon Topping, whisk together the eggs, sugar and lemon zest. Sift in the flour and baking powder, then add the lemon juice. Whisk together.

8. Pour the topping over the base and spread out evenly. Return it to the oven for a further 20 minutes, or until the topping doesn't jiggle.

9. Allow to cool to room temperature then chill until set before removing from the tin, dusting with the icing sugar and cutting into pieces.

10. Store in an airtight container in the fridge for up to 3 days.

Orange and Chocolate Chip Loaf

Another simple melt-and-mix loaf. The fresh orange juice and zest gives it a lovely citrus flavour that goes well with the dark chocolate chips. I like to serve it warm with butter spread on top, or a dollop of thick yoghurt.

---

175 g (6 oz) butter
1 cup white sugar
1 Tbsp finely grated orange zest
¼ cup orange juice
2 eggs, whisked
2 cups plain flour
2 tsp baking powder
1 cup dark chocolate chips

1. Preheat the oven to 170°C (325°F) fan bake.

2. Line a 27 x 13 cm (10¾ x 5 in) loaf tin with baking paper.

3. Melt the butter in a large glass bowl in the microwave. Add the sugar and whisk together. Stir in the orange zest and juice, then stir in the eggs.

4. Sift in the flour and baking powder. Add the chocolate chips and fold together until just combined.

5. Transfer to the lined loaf tin and bake for 50–60 minutes, or until a skewer inserted into the centre comes out clean.

6. Allow to cool in the tin for 20 minutes before transferring to a wire rack.

7. Store in an airtight container in the pantry for up to 3 days.

TIPS AND TRICKS

+ *Once cooled completely, this loaf can be frozen for up to 3 months. Wrap tightly in cling film to prevent freezer burn.*

Tropical Pineapple Cake with Cream Cheese Icing

I love the tropical combination of pineapple, lime and coconut in this cake — just thinking about it transports me to the islands. This recipe makes a light and fluffy cake that keeps well for a few days. Even though it doesn't have much height when you bake it, it will still have a great moist texture. Topped with everyone's favourite cream cheese icing, it's a real crowd-pleaser.

---

150 g (5½ oz) butter
1 cup white sugar
2 eggs
1 cup crushed pineapple, drained
½ cup desiccated coconut
2 Tbsp lime juice
1½ cups plain flour
2 tsp baking powder

CREAM CHEESE ICING
200 g (7 oz) cream cheese, softened
2 cups icing sugar
2 Tbsp crushed pineapple, drained
1 Tbsp lime zest
1 Tbsp lime juice

1. Preheat the oven to 170°C (325°F) fan bake.

2. Line a 22 cm (8½ in) round or square cake tin with baking paper.

3. Melt the butter in a large glass bowl in the microwave. Add the sugar and whisk together. Stir in the eggs. Add the pineapple, coconut and lime juice, then mix again.

4. Sift in the flour and baking powder, and fold together until just combined.

5. Transfer to the lined cake tin and bake for 45 minutes, or until a skewer inserted into the centre comes out clean. Allow to cool in the tin for 20 minutes before transferring to a wire rack.

6. To make the Cream Cheese Icing, whisk the cream cheese in a stand mixer or with hand-held beaters for 2 minutes. Add the icing sugar, pineapple, lime zest and lime juice, and beat until thick and creamy.

7. Spread the icing over the cooled cake and serve.

TIPS AND TRICKS

+ *If you don't like cream cheese, a standard lemon or lime icing would be delicious.*
+ *If you only have pineapple pieces or slices, blend them first.*

Lumberjack Cake

Everyone is so surprised by how good this cake tastes. It's a moist apple and date cake with a crunchy coconut topping. You bake the cake by itself first, then add the crunchy coconut topping and bake it again until it's golden and crispy. I like to serve it with a dollop of thick yoghurt, which complements the sweet, crunchy cake.

2 large apples, grated
1 cup dates, chopped
1 tsp baking soda
½ cup boiling water
125 g (4½ oz) butter
1 cup white sugar
1 egg
1 tsp vanilla essence
1½ cups plain flour
1 tsp baking powder
1 Tbsp icing sugar, to dust

CRUNCHY COCONUT TOPPING

60 g (2¼ oz) butter, melted
½ cup brown sugar
2 Tbsp milk
1 cup shredded coconut

TIPS AND TRICKS

+ *When returning the cake to the oven to crisp the topping, keep an eye on it. Every oven is a little different and you don't want it to burn.*

1. Preheat the oven to 180°C (350°F) fan bake.

2. Line a 22 cm (8½ in) diameter round cake tin with baking paper.

3. Place the apples, dates and baking soda in a bowl. Add the boiling water, mix together and set aside for 10 minutes while you make the batter.

4. Melt the butter in a large glass bowl in the microwave. Add the sugar and whisk together. Add the egg and vanilla and mix again.

5. Add the apple and date mixture and sift in the flour and baking powder. Fold together until just combined.

6. Transfer to the lined cake tin and bake for 55 minutes, or until the top springs back when you press it.

7. To make the Crunchy Coconut Topping, mix all the ingredients together in a bowl.

8. After 55 minutes, remove the cake from the oven and carefully spread the Crunchy Coconut Topping over the top. Return to the oven and bake for another 20 minutes until golden.

9. Allow to cool in the tin before turning out onto a serving plate and dusting with icing sugar to serve.

Easy Apple Cinnamon Scrolls with Vanilla Glaze

These cinnamon scrolls are a cross between a cinnamon bun and a scone. There isn't any yeast in the dough so you don't have to wait while they rise. Simply roll out the dough, spread with the filling, bake until golden, and drizzle with the yummy vanilla glaze topping.

---

50 g (1¾ oz) butter
¾ cup milk
2 cups plain flour
2 Tbsp brown sugar
1 Tbsp baking powder
½ tsp ground cinnamon

APPLE CINNAMON FILLING
¼ cup brown sugar
1 Tbsp ground cinnamon
385 g (13½ oz) can apple pieces
2 Tbsp butter, softened

VANILLA GLAZE
1 cup icing sugar
2 Tbsp milk
1 Tbsp butter, melted
1 tsp vanilla essence

1. Preheat the oven to 190°C (375°F) fan bake.

2. Line a 32 x 23 cm (12¾ x 9 in) baking dish with baking paper.

3. To make the dough, melt the butter in a large glass bowl in the microwave. Stir in the milk. Sift in the flour, sugar, baking powder and cinnamon, then fold together, adding a little extra milk if needed to bring together into a dough.

4. Turn out onto a floured bench, shape into a large ball and knead lightly for about 1 minute. Shape into a rectangle, then use a rolling pin dusted in flour to roll out to about 1 cm (½ in) thick.

5. To make the Apple Cinnamon Filling, mix the sugar and cinnamon. Drain the apples and chop coarsely. Spread the butter over the rolled-out dough, then sprinkle the cinnamon sugar and scatter the apples evenly over the top.

6. Roll up the dough tightly. Cut the roll into 12 even slices, then arrange the slices in the lined baking dish, leaving a little space between them. Bake for 20–25 minutes until cooked through and golden on top. Allow to cool slightly before glazing.

7. To make the Vanilla Glaze, whisk together all the ingredients in a small bowl. Drizzle the glaze over the warm scrolls. These are best served while they are still warm.

Mini Pizza Loaves

These pizza loaves look very cute with the mini pieces of salami on top. They're perfect for school lunches and they also freeze well. The mozzarella makes them light and fluffy. My kids love them, but they're not just for the kids — they're also a great addition to any shared morning tea.

1½ cups self-raising flour
1 cup grated mozzarella,
 plus extra for topping
50 g (1¾ oz) salami, diced
¼ cup finely chopped
 sun-dried tomatoes
4 eggs, whisked
½ cup milk
¼ cup olive oil
salt and cracked black
 pepper, to taste
1 mini salami stick, sliced

1. Preheat the oven to 180°C (350°F) fan bake.

2. Line 8–10 mini loaf tins with baking paper.

3. Stir together the flour, mozzarella, diced salami and sun-dried tomatoes in a large bowl.

4. Add the eggs, milk and olive oil. Season well with salt and pepper and stir together.

5. Spoon the mixture into the lined loaf tins. Top with extra mozzarella and slices of mini salami.

6. Bake for 18 minutes, or until the loaves are cooked through and a skewer inserted into the centre comes out clean. Allow to stand in the tins for 5 minutes before transferring to a wire rack to cool.

7. Serve warm with butter, or store in an airtight container in the fridge for up to 3 days.

TIPS AND TRICKS

+ *You can add extra cheese, ham, spring onion, olives, basil or parsley to suit your favourite flavours.*
+ *These are best frozen on the day they are made. Cool completely and then place in a sealable bag or wrap in cling film or tinfoil. Freeze for up to 1 month. Thaw in the fridge overnight or pop a frozen loaf into a lunchbox — it will thaw by lunchtime.*
+ *If you don't have mini loaf tins, a muffin tin will work fine, or this recipe can be made in one large loaf tin (note that cooking time may vary).*

Kids' fave

No-knead Rustic White Loaf

A simple, no-knead loaf that turns out just right every time, this is the perfect recipe to make when you have friends coming over for lunch. They'll be so impressed by your home-made bread coming out of the oven! I like to mix it the night before, knowing I'll have a beautiful dough ready to bake the next day.

---

5 cups plain, wholemeal or mixed-grain flour
1½ tsp salt
1½ tsp active dry yeast
2¼ cups warm water
2 Tbsp olive oil

TIPS AND TRICKS

+ *I use 3 cups plain flour and 2 cups mixed-grain flour, but you can use any combination.*
+ *A baking dish or ovenproof dish covered in tinfoil can be used instead of a cast-iron dish.*
+ *To make this in loaf tins, divide the dough in half, then roll each half into a loaf shape before placing in 2 loaf tins. Let the dough rise while the oven heats up to 210°C (410°F), then bake for 35 minutes uncovered.*

1. Place the flour, salt and yeast in a large bowl and whisk together.

2. Add the warm water and olive oil and mix together, scraping down the sides of the bowl as needed. Cover with a beeswax wrap, tea towel or cling film and allow to stand on the bench overnight or in a warm place for 6–24 hours.

3. When you are ready to bake your bread, place a cast-iron dish in the oven and preheat the oven to 220°C (425°F) fan bake.

4. Roughly shape the dough into a round on a sheet of baking paper and give it a light dusting of flour. Leave it on the bench to rise slightly while the oven heats up to temperature (about 20 minutes).

5. Slice a few lines in the top of the dough. Once the oven is up to temperature, remove the hot cast-iron dish from the oven, lift up the dough by its baking paper and place it in the dish.

6. Bake covered for 30 minutes, then remove the lid and bake for another 15 minutes until the loaf is cooked through and golden on top.

7. Serve warm with butter or toppings of your choice. This loaf is best eaten when fresh.

No-knead Seeded Bread

This wholesome seeded bread is made with wholemeal flour and a mixture of sunflower and pumpkin seeds, and you won't believe how easy it is. Simply mix it up the night before and you'll have a delicious dough to bake in the morning. It's perfect for toasting and also freezes well. If you do want to freeze it, I would suggest slicing it once cooled, then storing it in an old bread bag.

2 cups plain flour
2 cups wholemeal flour
½ cup rolled oats
3 Tbsp sunflower and/or pumpkin seeds
1 tsp salt
1 tsp active dry yeast
2¼ cups warm water

1. Place the plain flour, wholemeal flour, rolled oats, seeds, salt and yeast in a large bowl and whisk together.

2. Add the warm water and mix together, scraping down the sides of the bowl as needed. Cover with a beeswax wrap, tea towel or cling film and allow to stand on the bench overnight or in a warm place for 6–24 hours.

3. When you are ready to bake your bread, preheat the oven to 200°C (400°F) fan bake.

4. Oil a 19 x 11.5 cm (7½ x 5¾ in) loaf tin. Roughly shape the dough into an oval, then add to the oiled loaf tin. Leave it on the bench to rise slightly while the oven heats up to temperature (about 20 minutes).

5. Bake for 40 minutes until the loaf is cooked through and golden on top.

6. Serve warm with butter or toppings of your choice.

TIPS AND TRICKS

+ *Feel free to mix up the seeds. You could add sesame seeds, poppy seeds or linseeds to the mix, or even sprinkle some on top if you like.*

Classic Focaccia Bread

Nothing beats warm focaccia bread coming out of the oven. I love to dip it in olive oil and dukkah. It is also perfect served with my Tuscan chicken (see page 52) to mop up that delicious sauce. This is a very versatile recipe, which you can jazz up with olives, feta or your favourite herbs.

1 cup warm water
1 tsp sugar
1 tsp active dry yeast
2½ cups high-grade flour
1 tsp salt
4 Tbsp olive oil
1 Tbsp fresh rosemary, chopped
1½ tsp flaky sea salt

TIPS AND TRICKS

+ Parmesan, pesto and sun-dried tomatoes would all make good topping additions.

+ When poking holes in the bread, I use both hands and all my fingers and move from one end of the dish to the other. It kind of looks like you're playing the piano on the bread.

1. Place warm water and sugar in a large bowl or the bowl of a stand mixer and stir to dissolve.

2. Add the yeast and stir again. Cover with a tea towel and allow to stand for 10 minutes.

3. Add the flour, salt and 3 tablespoons of the olive oil and stir together. Knead with a dough hook or by hand for 5 minutes until smooth and a little sticky.

4. Cover with a tea towel and allow to rise in a warm place for 30 minutes.

5. Thoroughly grease a large baking tray with cooking spray or olive oil.

6. Place the dough in the centre of the tray and push it out to the edges with your hands. Drizzle the last tablespoon of olive oil over the dough mix, making sure it is all covered.

7. Using your fingers, poke dimples in the top of the dough. Scatter with the rosemary and flaky sea salt.

8. Preheat the oven to 200°C (400°F) fan bake and leave the dough to rise for 20 minutes while the oven comes to temperature.

9. Bake for 20 minutes until cooked through and golden on top.

Sweet Treats

What's in this Chapter

PEPPERMINT WEET-BIX SLICE • PAGE 158

BLUEBERRY AND APPLE CRUMBLE SLICE • PAGE 160

CHOCOLATE CHIP SPRINKLE COOKIES • PAGE 162

DARK CHOCOLATE, PEANUT BUTTER AND CARAMEL BROWNIE • PAGE 164

APRICOT MUESLI BAR SLICE • PAGE 166

DOUBLE CHOCOLATE COOKIES • PAGE 168

LEMON WEET-BIX SLICE • PAGE 170

RASPBERRY CHEESECAKE BROWNIE • PAGE 172

CRANBERRY MAGIC SLICE • PAGE 174

Peppermint Weet-Bix Slice

This is a twist on my website's most popular recipe of all time — Chocolate Weet-Bix Slice. After making it for years, I decided it was time to mix things up with a peppermint icing. I've included both versions here so you can make them and decide which one is your favourite.

---

185 g (6½ oz) butter
1 cup white sugar
2 Tbsp cocoa
3 Weet-Bix, crushed
1 cup plain flour
1 cup desiccated coconut
1 tsp baking powder

PEPPERMINT ICING
2½ cups icing sugar
1½ tsp peppermint essence
50 g (1¾ oz) butter, melted
3–4 Tbsp boiling water
1 drop green food colouring
 (optional)

CHOCOLATE DRIZZLE
(OPTIONAL)
50 g (1¾ oz) milk chocolate
1 tsp vegetable oil

TIPS AND TRICKS
+ *To make Classic Chocolate Icing instead, whisk 2 cups icing sugar, 3 Tbsp cocoa, 50 g (1¾ oz) softened butter and 2–3 Tbsp of boiling water until smooth.*

1. Preheat the oven to 180°C (350°F) fan bake.

2. Line a 27 x 17 cm (10½ x 6½ in) slice tin with baking paper.

3. Melt together the butter, sugar and cocoa in a large pot over a low heat. Remove from the heat then add the Weet-Bix, flour, coconut and baking powder. Mix together.

4. Transfer to the lined slice tin and press out evenly.

5. Bake for 14–18 minutes until the slice is cooked but feels soft to the touch in the centre. It will firm up as it cools.

6. To make the Peppermint Icing, mix the icing sugar, peppermint essence and melted butter. Add the boiling water as needed to loosen the mixture, and whisk until there are no lumps. Add a drop of food colouring if you want to make the icing minty green.

7. If making the Chocolate Drizzle, melt the chocolate in the microwave in 15-second bursts, stirring well each time. Don't let it get too hot or it might split and ruin your chocolate. Stir in the oil and whisk until smooth. Transfer to a small piping bag made from baking paper or a sealable bag with the corner snipped off.

8. Spread the icing over the base while it is still warm. Allow to cool and set before removing from the tin, cutting into pieces and adding the Chocolate Drizzle, if desired.

Kids' fave

Blueberry and Apple Crumble Slice

This apple crumble slice is so easy to make and has a nice crunch to it. You can use any berries that you have on hand, but I love the combination of blueberries and apples. I always have frozen blueberries in the freezer.

2 cups plain flour
1 cup white sugar
1 tsp baking powder
1 tsp ground cinnamon
1 egg
150 g (5½ oz) butter, melted, plus 30 g (1 oz) extra for topping
1 tsp vanilla essence
2 apples
1½ cups frozen blueberries
½ cup rolled oats

TIPS AND TRICKS

+ *You don't need to defrost the berries first. I place them on a paper towel to catch any excess liquid while I make the base. You can also use fresh berries if they are in season.*

1. Preheat the oven to 170°C (325°F) fan bake.

2. Line a 27 x 17 cm (10½ x 6½ in) slice tin with baking paper.

3. Whisk together the flour, sugar, baking powder and cinnamon in a large bowl.

4. Add the egg, melted butter and vanilla, and mix together until you can no longer see white bits of flour.

5. Set aside 1 cup of mixture for the topping. Transfer the rest to the lined slice tin and press out evenly, smoothing the top with the back of a metal spoon.

6. Peel the apples and cut into 1 cm (½ in) dice. Spread evenly over the base, then do the same with the blueberries.

7. Add the reserved 1 cup of topping mix back to the bowl. Add the rolled oats and the extra 30 g (1 oz) of melted butter, and mix together with a spoon or press together with your hands.

8. Crumble the topping over the apple and blueberries, pressing down gently with your hands.

9. Bake for 45–50 minutes until cooked through and golden on top.

10. Allow to cool before removing from the tin and cutting into pieces. Serve at room temperature.

Chocolate Chip Sprinkle Cookies

This recipe is based on the 'Kiwi crisp cookies' that Mike's grandma Miggs used to make. Sweetened condensed milk cookies have been around in New Zealand for generations, and here I've added some sprinkles and chocolate chips to brighten them up. They last for days and are definitely a family favourite.

150 g (5½ oz) butter, softened

½ cup brown sugar, firmly packed

150 g (5½ oz) sweetened condensed milk

1 tsp vanilla essence

2 cups plain flour

2 tsp baking powder

100 g (3½ oz) chocolate chips

3 Tbsp sprinkles

TIPS AND TRICKS

+ *I used my ice cream scoop to roll the dough into balls. You can also use a tablespoon.*

+ *Freeze any extra balls of cookie dough in a sealable bag or an airtight container for up to 3 months.*

1. Preheat the oven to 170°C (325°F) fan bake.

2. Line 2 baking trays with baking paper.

3. Cream the butter and sugar together in a stand mixer or with hand-held beaters until light and fluffy.

4. Add the condensed milk and vanilla, then mix on high speed until light and fluffy.

5. Sift in the flour and baking powder, then add the chocolate chips and sprinkles and mix together until combined.

6. Roll the dough into balls of about 2 tablespoons each, and place on the lined baking trays. Flatten with the palm of your hand.

7. Bake for 12 minutes or until just starting to brown.

8. Allow to cool on the trays for 5 minutes before transfering to a wire rack.

9. Store in an airtight container in the pantry for up to a week.

Kids' fave

Dark Chocolate, Peanut Butter and Caramel Brownie

I love a fudgy and gooey brownie, and this version, topped with peanut butter and caramel, is one of my all-time favourites. I've used canned caramel so it's quick to make. Just drizzle it over the top and bake until it's cooked to your liking.

---

100 g (3½ oz) dark chocolate
100 g (3½ oz) butter
½ cup plain flour
⅓ cup cocoa
1 tsp baking powder
1 cup white sugar
2 eggs, lightly whisked
100 g (3½ oz) caramel condensed milk
2 Tbsp smooth peanut butter

1. Preheat the oven to 180°C (350°F) fan bake.

2. Line a 20 cm (8 in) square slice tin with baking paper.

3. Gently melt together the chocolate and butter in a large pot or in a large glass bowl in the microwave. Stir until smooth.

4. Sift in the flour, cocoa and baking powder. Add the sugar and eggs, then mix together until combined.

5. Transfer to the lined slice tin and spread out evenly.

6. Whisk together the condensed milk and peanut butter until combined. Dot over the brownie batter, then run a skewer through to swirl it around.

7. Bake for 25–30 minutes until it feels firm on the surface.

8. Allow to cool before removing from the tin and cutting into pieces.

9. Store in an airtight container in the pantry for up to 3 days.

TIPS AND TRICKS

+ *This brownie can be made without the caramel and peanut butter if you want a plain brownie.*
+ *You could add berries or chocolate chunks.*

Apricot Muesli Bar Slice

If you get sick of buying muesli bars for the kids' lunchboxes,
this apricot slice is a great one to make. The honey gives it
a beautiful flavour and you can swap the dried apricots for
any dried fruit, such as dried cranberries or raisins.

1 cup rolled oats
½ cup desiccated coconut
½ cup brown sugar
¼ cup self-raising flour
½ tsp ground cinnamon
125 g (4½ oz) butter
¼ cup honey
2 eggs, whisked
½ cup chocolate chips
½ cup dried apricots,
  chopped

1. Preheat the oven to 170°C (325°F) fan bake.

2. Line a 27 x 17 cm (10½ x 6½ in) slice tin with baking paper.

3. Stir together the rolled oats, coconut, sugar, flour and
   cinnamon in a large bowl.

4. Melt the butter and honey in a small glass jug in the
   microwave. Add to the dry ingredients along with the eggs
   and mix together. Stir in the chocolate chips and apricots.

5. Transfer to the lined slice tin and press out evenly.

6. Bake for 20–25 minutes until cooked through and golden
   on top.

7. Allow to cool before removing from the tin and cutting
   into bars.

8. Store in an airtight container in the pantry for up to
   a week.

Kids'
fave

Double Chocolate Cookies

These decadent double chocolate cookies are the perfect combination of chewy and crispy, and delicious served warm with a glass of milk. They almost seem like a fudgy brownie! They are quick to make and I love to have a bag of cookie dough balls in the freezer so I can bake cookies at the last minute for the family. I add extra chocolate drops after they've been cooked so they look amazing.

150 g (5½ oz) butter
½ cup brown sugar
½ cup white sugar
1 egg
1 tsp vanilla essence
1¾ cups plain flour
½ cup cocoa
1 Tbsp cornflour
1 tsp baking soda
¼ tsp salt
1 cup milk chocolate drops

TIPS AND TRICKS

+ *Freeze any extra balls of cookie dough in a sealable bag or airtight container for up to 3 months.*

1. Preheat the oven to 170°C (325°F) fan bake.

2. Line 2 baking trays with baking paper.

3. Melt the butter in a large glass bowl in the microwave. Add the sugars and whisk together. Add the egg and vanilla and mix until there are no lumps.

4. Sift in the flour, cocoa, cornflour, baking soda and salt, and fold together until combined.

5. Stir in ¾ cup of the chocolate drops, reserving the rest to garnish.

6. Roll the dough into balls of about 2 tablespoons each and place on the lined baking trays. Flatten with the palm of your hand.

7. Bake for 8–10 minutes until turning crispy on the outside but still very soft in the centre. Arrange extra chocolate drops on top while they are still hot.

8. Allow to cool on the trays for a few minutes before transferring to a wire rack.

9. Store in an airtight container in the pantry for up to a week.

Lemon Weet-Bix Slice

After the popularity of my chocolate Weet-Bix slice (see page 158)
I thought I would make a delicious lemon version. This slice has a
chewy coconut and Weet-Bix base that goes so well with the tangy and
delicious lemon icing. I wonder which version will be your favourite?

185 g (6½ oz) butter, melted
1 cup white sugar
3 Weet-Bix, crushed
1 cup plain flour
1 cup desiccated coconut
1 tsp baking powder

ZESTY ICING
2 cups icing sugar
50 g (1¾ oz) butter, melted
2 tsp finely grated lemon
   zest
¼ cup lemon juice

1. Preheat the oven to 180°C (350°F) fan bake.

2. Line a 27 x 17 cm (10½ x 6½ in) slice tin with baking paper.

3. Melt the butter in a large glass bowl in the microwave. Add
   the sugar and whisk together. Add the Weet-Bix, flour,
   coconut and baking powder and mix together.

4. Transfer to the lined slice tin and press out evenly.

5. Bake for 15–20 minutes until it is cooked through but soft
   to touch. It will firm up as it cools.

6. To make the Zesty Icing, mix together the icing sugar,
   butter and lemon zest and juice. Add a little boiling water
   if needed to loosen the mixture, and whisk until there are
   no lumps.

7. Spread the icing over the base while it is still warm. Allow
   to cool and set before removing from the tin and cutting
   into pieces.

8. Store in an airtight container in the fridge or a cool, dry
   place for up to 4 days.

TIPS AND TRICKS

+ *I often use the crumbs at the bottom of the Weet-Bix box for
  this slice. You'll need about 50 g (1¾ oz) of crumbs to make up
  the 3 Weet-Bix.*

+ *To make a Passionfruit Weet-Bix Slice, swap the lemon juice
  and zest in the icing for the pulp of 3 passionfruit.*

Kids'
fave

Raspberry Cheesecake Brownie

After trying a raspberry cheesecake brownie in a café years ago I thought it was about time I made one myself. This one is so good, with the simple mix-together brownie topped with a beautiful cream cheese topping. Pop the raspberries in and it adds a nice tart flavour to offset the creamy cheesecake. You can use any type of frozen berries.

---

100 g (3½ oz) butter
1 cup brown sugar
¼ cup cocoa
2 eggs
1 cup self-raising flour
250 g (9 oz) cream cheese, softened
½ cup caster sugar
1 tsp vanilla essence
55 g (2 oz) frozen raspberries

1. Preheat the oven to 170°C (325°F) fan bake.

2. Line a 20 cm (8 in) square slice tin with baking paper.

3. Melt the butter in a large glass bowl in the microwave. Add the brown sugar and whisk together.

4. Add the cocoa and 1 egg, whisking well after each addition. Sift in the flour and fold together until combined.

5. Transfer to the lined slice tin and spread out evenly.

6. Whip the cream cheese, caster sugar, vanilla and the remaining egg in a stand mixer or with hand-held beaters until well combined. Pour evenly over the brownie base. Dot the frozen raspberries on top, pushing them into the mixture as you go.

7. Bake for 35 minutes until the cream cheese topping is almost set.

8. Allow to cool to room temperature, then chill for 2 hours or overnight before removing from the tin and cutting into pieces.

9. Store in an airtight container in the fridge for up to 4 days.

Cranberry Magic Slice

Everyone is so surprised by how delicious this magic slice is! You start off with a biscuit base and add layers of chocolate, coconut, cranberries, seeds and nuts, then pour over the sweetened condensed milk and bake until it's golden. It's so tasty and another great lunchbox filler.

---

250 g (9 oz) packet Krispie biscuits
175 g (6 oz) butter, melted
1 cup dark chocolate chips
1 cup shredded coconut
1 cup chopped dried cranberries
½ cup sunflower seeds
½ cup slivered almonds
395 g (14 oz) sweetened condensed milk

1. Preheat the oven to 170°C (325°F) fan bake.

2. Line a 27 x 17 cm (10½ x 6½ in) slice tin with baking paper.

3. Crush the biscuits in a food processor. Add the melted butter and pulse until combined.

4. Transfer to the lined slice tin and spread out evenly, smoothing the top with the back of a metal spoon.

5. Scatter the chocolate chips, coconut, dried cranberries, sunflower seeds and almonds in even layers over the top, then pour over the condensed milk.

6. Bake for 25–35 minutes until golden.

7. Allow to cool to room temperature, then chill until set before removing from the tin and cutting into pieces.

8. Store in an airtight container in the fridge for up to a week.

TIPS AND TRICKS

+ *Any plain biscuits such as Milk Arrowroot, Super Wine or Malt biscuits work in this recipe.*

+ *If you don't have a food processor, place the biscuits in a large sealable bag and crush them with a rolling pin.*

Gingernut Slice

This no-bake slice is another goodie! Using the classic Gingernuts
in the base and topped with a ginger icing, it's easy and
delicious. If you're a ginger fan, this slice is the one for you.

---

250 g (9 oz) packet
  Gingernut biscuits
80 g (2¾ oz) butter
80 g (2¾ oz) sweetened
  condensed milk

GINGER ICING
50 g (1¾ oz) butter
1 Tbsp golden syrup
¾ cup icing sugar
1 Tbsp ground ginger

1. Line a 20 cm (8 in) square slice tin with baking paper.

2. Crush the biscuits in a food processor.

3. Melt the butter and condensed milk in a large glass bowl
   in the microwave, then whisk together. Stir in the crushed
   biscuits.

4. Transfer to the lined slice tin and press out evenly,
   smoothing the top with the back of a metal spoon. Chill
   the base in the freezer while you make the icing.

5. To make the Ginger Icing, melt the butter and golden
   syrup in the microwave, then mix together. Sift in the icing
   sugar and ginger, then whisk together until smooth.

6. Spread the icing over the chilled base.

7. Chill for 3 hours until set. Remove from the fridge
   20 minutes before cutting into pieces (this makes it easier
   to cut).

8. Store in an airtight container in the fridge for up to a week.

TIPS AND TRICKS

+ *If you don't have a food processor, place the biscuits in a
  large sealable bag and crush them with a rolling pin.*
+ *If your icing is too thick, add a teaspoon of boiling water to
  make it more spreadable. If your icing is too runny, add extra
  icing sugar.*

Rainbow Slice

This easy and colourful rainbow slice is perfect for children's birthday parties. It's such fun to make with the kids. My boys love putting on the rows of Smarties.

250 g (9 oz) packet Milk
 Arrowroot biscuits
150 g (5½ oz) butter
200 g (7 oz) dark chocolate
200 g (7 oz) sweetened
 condensed milk
1 cup rice bubbles

RAINBOW TOPPING
250 g (9 oz) white
 chocolate
1 Tbsp vegetable oil
120 g (4½ oz) Smarties
2 Tbsp sprinkles

1. Line a 27 x 17 cm (10½ x 6½ in) slice tin with baking paper.

2. Crush the biscuits in a food processor.

3. Gently melt together the butter, chocolate and condensed milk in a large pot or in a large glass bowl in the microwave. Stir until smooth.

4. Stir in the crushed biscuits and rice bubbles.

5. Transfer to the lined slice tin and press out evenly, smoothing the top with the back of a metal spoon.

6. To make the Rainbow Topping, carefully melt the white chocolate in the microwave, add the oil and stir until smooth. Pour over the base and spread out evenly. Arrange the Smarties in lines of each colour, then scatter with sprinkles.

7. Chill for at least 4 hours until set. Remove from the fridge 20 minutes before cutting into pieces (this makes it easier to cut).

8. Store in an airtight container in the fridge for up to a week.

TIPS AND TRICKS
+ *You can use any plain biscuits, such as Super Wine, Milk Arrowroot or Marie biscuits.*
+ *If you don't have a food processor, place the biscuits in a large sealable bag and crush them with a rolling pin.*
+ *To speed up the setting process you can chill the slice in the freezer for 30 minutes.*

Kids' fave

Easy Caramilk Blondies

Everyone goes crazy for Caramilk, and this slice is a great way to use it. It's easy to make and so delicious and indulgent. Dust with icing sugar at the end, and serve with a cup of tea or coffee.

---

100 g (3½ oz) butter
180 g (6½ oz) Caramilk chocolate
1 cup brown sugar
¾ cup plain flour
1 tsp baking powder
2 eggs, lightly whisked
1 Tbsp icing sugar, to dust

1. Preheat the oven to 180°C (350°F) fan bake.

2. Line a 20 cm (8 in) square slice tin with baking paper.

3. Gently melt together the butter and 100 g (3½ oz) of the chocolate in a large pot over a low heat or in a large glass bowl in the microwave. Add the sugar and stir until smooth.

4. Remove from the heat and sift in the flour and baking powder.

5. Chop the remaining 80 g (2¾ oz) of chocolate into chunks, then add to the mixture with the whisked eggs. Mix everything together.

6. Transfer to the lined slice tin and spread out evenly.

7. Bake for 25–30 minutes until it feels firm on the surface.

8. Allow to cool before removing from the tin, dusting with icing sugar and cutting into pieces.

TIPS AND TRICKS

+ *Be sure to heat the chocolate and butter gently. If the heat is too high it might split.*
+ *White chocolate could be used instead of the Caramilk if you prefer.*

Belgian Slice

My version of Belgian Slice is a twist on the classic cookies. It has a spiced melt-and-mix base and is topped with a bright pink raspberry icing. It looks so impressive and is perfect for a morning tea with friends.

---

175 g (6 oz) butter
½ cup brown sugar
3 Tbsp golden syrup
1 egg, whisked
1½ cups plain flour
1 tsp baking powder
2 tsp ground cinnamon
1 Tbsp mixed spice

RASPBERRY JELLY ICING
2 Tbsp raspberry jelly crystals, plus 1 Tbsp to garnish
2 Tbsp boiling water
3 Tbsp raspberry jam
2 cups icing sugar

1. Preheat the oven to 170°C (325°F) fan bake.

2. Line a 27 x 17 cm (10½ x 6½ in) slice tin with baking paper.

3. Melt the butter in a large glass bowl in the microwave. Add the sugar and golden syrup and whisk together. Add the egg and mix again.

4. Sift in the flour, baking powder, cinnamon and mixed spice, and mix together well.

5. Transfer to the lined slice tin, spread out evenly and bake for 20 minutes.

6. To make the Raspberry Jelly Icing, place the jelly crystals in a bowl, then add the boiling water and whisk together. Add the raspberry jam and whisk again. Sift in the icing sugar and mix together.

7. Spread the icing over the base while it is still warm, then sprinkle with the extra 1 tablespoon of jelly crystals.

8. Chill until set before removing from the tin and cutting into pieces with a sharp knife.

9. Store in an airtight container in the pantry for up to 4 days.

Huge Oaty Chocolate Chunk Cookies

This recipe makes a huge batch of cookies, so I like to freeze half the dough for later. I also sprinkle over extra chopped chocolate at the end so it melts into the hot cookies. Swap the chocolate for any of your favourites, such as chocolate chips, pecans, sprinkles, peanuts or M&Ms.

300 g (10½ oz) softened butter

1 cup brown sugar

1 cup caster sugar

2 eggs

2 tsp vanilla essence

3 cups plain flour

1 tsp ground cinnamon

1 tsp baking soda

¼ cup milk

1 cup rolled oats

200 g (7 oz) chocolate, coarsely chopped

TIPS AND TRICKS

+ *If you don't chill the dough before baking they will spread very quickly, so give them lots of space on the trays.*

+ *If you want to freeze half the mix for later, you can put the rolled-up cookie dough balls in a sealable bag once they are frozen.*

1. Cream the butter and sugars together in a stand mixer or with hand-held beaters until light and fluffy. Add the eggs and vanilla, then mix again until well combined.

2. Sift in the flour, cinnamon and baking soda. Add the milk, then mix on low speed until just combined.

3. Add the rolled oats and chopped chocolate, reserving a tablespoon of the chocolate to garnish. Stir together.

4. Use a dough scoop or ice cream scoop to roll the dough into 24 balls. Chill the cookie dough balls in the freezer for at least 20 minutes.

5. Preheat the oven to 170°C (325°F) fan bake.

6. Line 2 baking trays with baking paper.

7. Arrange the chilled dough balls on the lined baking trays, leaving lots of space between them. Bake for 15–20 minutes until turning golden but still soft in the centre.

8. Sprinkle the reserved chocolate over the cookies when they come out of the oven.

9. Store in an airtight container in the pantry for up to a week.

Sticky Date and Caramel Slice

One of my all-time favourite desserts is sticky date pudding, and I thought it was time I made a slice that combines the flavours of dates with a creamy caramel golden syrup icing. Something different that you probably haven't tried before!

175 g (6 oz) butter
½ cup brown sugar
150 g (5½ oz) dates, chopped
1½ cups plain flour
1 tsp baking powder
¼ tsp salt
1 egg, whisked

CARAMEL ICING
50 g (1¾ oz) butter
3 Tbsp golden syrup
1 cup icing sugar

1. Preheat the oven to 180°C (350°F) fan bake.

2. Line a 20 cm (8 in) square slice tin with baking paper.

3. Melt the butter and sugar in a large pot over a low heat. Add the dates and cook, stirring, for 3 minutes until the dates soften.

4. Sift in the flour, baking powder and salt. Add the egg, and mix together until just combined.

5. Transfer to the lined slice tin and press out evenly, smoothing the top with the back of a metal spoon.

6. Bake for 15 minutes until golden on top. Allow to cool for 10 minutes before icing.

7. To make the Caramel Icing, melt together the butter and golden syrup, sift in the icing sugar, and whisk until there are no lumps.

8. Spread the icing over the base while it is still warm. Allow to cool and set before removing from the tin and cutting into pieces.

9. Store in an airtight container in the pantry for up to a week.

Acknowledgements

Firstly, I want to thank all my followers on Instagram and Facebook: you guys are the ones who made this happen. I can't believe that my journey has led me here and that I have a real-life book in print! I am so happy with the way it turned out.

A huge thank you to Michelle and the team at Allen & Unwin for believing in me when I pitched my idea for a family-friendly cookbook. Thanks so much for having faith in me and trusting that this could come to fruition. I'm so glad you did. It was quite a process but look at what we have made.

Next up, I have to mention the dream team: photographer Mel Jenkins and food stylist Jo Bridgford, who brought all of my recipes to life with gorgeous styling and photography. You are both so talented at what you do, and the result is sensational.

Thanks so much to my husband, Mikey, for supporting me through this whole food-blogging ride. You have been my rock and have always believed in me, despite all my crazy ideas and the late nights that I put in. You know that I'm working towards an awesome goal. Thanks so much for being there for me.

Thanks to my sons, Archie and Henry, for being my chief taste-testers and for your *complete* honesty when giving me your verdict on each recipe. All kids have different tastes, and my two certainly aren't afraid to tell me what they think!

Thanks to my mum, sisters and family for sharing my Facebook posts over the years, spamming their friends with my recipes and generally being my biggest supporters.

I couldn't have done this without my right-hand gal Theresa Reddish, who has been with me for three years now, working on the website as well as brainstorming, typing and testing the recipes for the cookbook, especially on our cookathon days! You are incredible and so good at what you do; I really appreciate all the help you have given me.

Thanks to the rest of the VJ Cooks team, including my sister Holly Bowen for proofing the manuscript, doing email marketing, being my membership manager and keeping everything running smoothly; my sister Grace Bowen for helping me come up with recipes when I need inspiration and brainstorming like a champion; and Erin Sinclair for helping me out on shoot days, creating recipes, looking after my Facebook page and being chief dishwasher.

I am grateful to Jane Binsley for editing the cookbook and whipping my words into shape. I'm a designer, not a writer, and Jane has made sure that the recipes are clear, consistent and easy to follow. Thanks also to the proofreaders and indexer for your careful work.

Thanks to Kate Barraclough, who did the design for the cookbook. It's so nice to hand the design over to someone else and trust that they will make it look wonderful.

Thanks to Melle van Sambeek, a long-time friend from my magazine days, for doing my hair and makeup for the cover shoot and lifestyle shots.

A huge thanks goes out to my food-blogger friends, who inspire me every day and are always there for me when I need them: Anna Cameron from Just a Mum, Jana MacPherson from The MacPherson Diaries, Laura MacDonald from The Kiwi Country Girl, and Philippa Cameron from What's for Smoko. You guys are the best, and I love that we're all about building each other up and sharing ideas. Thanks also to the wider community of food bloggers who motivate me every day; it's fascinating to follow along with your journeys.

There are so many other people I would like to acknowledge but the list could go on and on, so I will just say a general thank you to everyone who has played a part along the way. You know who you are, and I hope you know how grateful I am.

Vanya

Index

Note: Vanya uses New Zealand standard measures, including the 15 ml (3 teaspoon) tablespoon. If you are using the Australian 20 ml (4 teaspoon) tablespoon, you may wish to remove a teaspoon of ingredient for each tablespoon specified.

First published in 2022

Text © Vanya Insull, 2022
Photography © Melanie Jenkins (Flash Studios), 2022
Styling by Jo Bridgford (Delivision Food Styling)

Allen & Unwin
Level 2, 10 College Hill, Freemans Bay
Auckland 1011, New Zealand
Phone: (64 9) 377 3800
Email: auckland@allenandunwin.com
Web: www.allenandunwin.co.nz

83 Alexander Street
Crows Nest NSW 2065, Australia
Phone: (61 2) 8425 0100

A catalogue record for this book is available from the National Library of New Zealand.

ISBN 978 1 99100 605 9

Design by Kate Barraclough
Set in Brown
Printed in China by C & C Offset Printing Co., Ltd.

10 9 8 7 6 5 4 3 2